DATE DUE

ORGANIZE YOUR OFFICE!

SIMPLE ROUTINES FOR MANAGING YOUR WORKSPACE

ORGANIZE YOUR OFFICE!

SIMPLE ROUTINES
FOR MANAGING
YOUR WORKSPACE

RONNI EISENBERG WITH KATE KELLY

HYPERION
NEW YORK

ISBN 0-7868-8381-2

Revised Edition

10 9 8 7

Design by Robert Bull Design

CONTENTS

Introduction

Here are Ten Simple Steps to an Organized Office

1. Create a good calendar system and don't leave your office without it.

2. Items to do? Write them *all* down so you don't forget.

3. Always tackle the most important task first.

4. When your day is careening out of control, ask: What is most important for me to do now? By assessing what *needs* to get done and what can wait, you can automatically prioritize.

5. Important project due, and you've had it with distractions? Remove yourself. Find a quiet conference room and close the door.

6. Can't get started? Break the project down into small steps that can be accomplished in short time slots.

7. Process your mail on a day-to-day basis so it doesn't pile up.

8. Set up a simple filing system that gets papers off your desk and stored away. Never pile! When you start a new project, give it a labeled folder of its own.

9. Always refile what you take out.

10. Take ten minutes to organize your desk before you go home, and lay out your top priority for the next day. You'll start work with a clean desk and a clear mind.

ORGANIZE YOUR OFFICE!

SIMPLE ROUTINES
FOR MANAGING
YOUR WORKSPACE

PART ONE

TIME

MANAGEMENT

1
CALENDARS

WHAT'S AHEAD

General Pointers
Paper or Computer?
Calendar Tips
**Electronic Calendars
and Personal Digital Assistants**

A friend of mine, a real estate agent, used to have a dreadful time keeping track of her appointments. She eventually arrived, but sometimes it was at the wrong place, and often it was the wrong time. The problem? Her calendar!

If you made a date with her, you generally had to repeat information twice: today, and a week later because she never wrote it down the first time. And when she did write things down, her notes ran up one side of the calendar and down the other with arrows and stars to mark the way.

I offered her several wonderful calendar systems, pleading with her to give them a try. My pleas fell on deaf ears until one night she arrived at her company banquet in a limousine she'd hired for the occasion. She'd just had her hair done and purchased a new dress and shoes for the event. She was set for the perfect evening—one night too early!

Several days later she called me explaining with excitement that she'd finally tried one of the new calendars. "I wish I'd done it sooner," she confessed. "I can keep track of so many things, and I know my life will be easier. I'll be able to get things done, and I'll always know where I'm supposed to be—and get it right the first time around!"

GENERAL POINTERS

Today's business person has more calendars than ever to choose from. Whether you're looking for a paper, software, or electronic-style calendar, there are several points to keep in mind:

- The best calendar functions as a complete scheduling companion, with space for a daily "to do" list, reminders of everything from birthdays to business meetings, and room for at least a small telephone directory. In addition, most people like to have a diary section for work accomplished and work-related expenses.

- The paper system I favor has a two-page spread for each day with a month-at-a-glance system in the back that allows you to plan ahead. There is space for notes, expenses, and work accomplished.

- If you are considering a calendar system for your computer, tell the salesperson or computer consultant which paper calendar system you favor. Some of the most popular ones have had software designed to mimic them.

- When possible, plan to use only one calendar; with more than one, there is always the risk of forgetting to keep both up to date. Executives with secretaries may require two. I generally recommend that the secretary's desk feature a desk calendar; the executive should then work from a smaller, more portable style.

- Because you're not always at your desk, your calendar needs to be portable. People who opt for a computer-based calendar system (and don't carry notebook-size computers with them), should take along a print-out of their calendar when they are away from the office.

- What's your backup? With a computer or an electronic system, you need to be certain you have a print-out or, preferably, a backup copy of your calendar. But this is also true of a paper calendar. What if you lose it? Pages from a telephone directory should be photocopied annually, and at times when you're out of the office a great deal (increasing the possibility of loss), make a photocopy of your most important calendar pages—those with a good number of notes and appointments yet to come.

- Don't remain wedded to a system that doesn't work for you. A new job may mean more appointments, and your calendar may not have space for all you need to note down—switch calendars, even if it's midyear.

CALENDAR TIPS

- Keep your calendar on your desk, open and available so that you can easily see what awaits you.

- Write down everything. You may have a department meeting every Thursday afternoon that "you'll never forget." But if you haven't written it down and someone asks for an appointment, it's easy to forget that Thursday afternoon is booked.

- If you use more than one calendar (one on your desk, one on your secretary's), *all appointments must be noted on both calendars*. At your daily meeting, double-check that all entries are correct, and if the secretary books anything during the day, he or she should be certain to note it on the executive's calendar immediately.

PAPER OR COMPUTER?

■ Undecided as to whether to stay with your paper calendar or try a computerized one? Paper-based calendars are still easiest for noting down an idle thought about a project; they are always "on"; and most styles are portable. On the other hand, electronic calendars and software calendar programs offer amazing capabilities:

❑ alarm reminders

❑ warning system for overlapping commitments

❑ search capabilities for specific information

❑ auto-dialing from your computerized phone directory and faxing

❑ time analysis (a time log with summary)

❑ ability to carry forward undone "to do" items

❑ group scheduling

❑ scheduling from two locations (your secretary can schedule directly into your computerized calendar)

❑ rescheduling ease: if your 3:00 P.M. client meeting must be rescheduled for the following week, you need only enter a stroke or two, and all the information you needed for the meeting (place, directions, items to take) jumps to the new date

- If a secretary or assistant books some of your time, discuss leaving time free (such as mornings for priority work) so you're not wall-to-wall with appointments.

- When you record an appointment, write down the address, telephone number, and directions in the space next to the appointment. That way you have the phone number handy if you have to reschedule, and because you noted all the information the first time, you needn't call back for directions.

WORTH THE TIME

- Write urgent "to do" items in red.

- Always review your activities a week in advance so that you can plan around your existing appointments.

- Make appointments with yourself (and note them on your calendar). Sometimes this is the only way to be sure that you have time to get a specific project done.

- For the hard-to-get-hold-of: book a phone appointment and write that down.

- Check your calendar every day. (For better planning, do it the night before when you create your "to do" list.) You'd be surprised at how many people forget to look at their schedule before making plans.

Electric Organizers and Personal Digital Assistants

If you envy your co-workers who are punching in appointments and telephone numbers into their electronic organizers or palmtop computers, then perhaps it's time for you to move into the electronic age. The electronic organizers have many capabilities that can't be duplicated with paper-based systems: In addition to serving as calendar and telephone directory, they can act as an alarm clock, pager, calculator, note pad, expense log, game board, e-mail retrieval system and Web browser.

The organizers/computers come in two basic models: One style, the **personal information manager**, is a hand-held electronic device designed to keep phone lists, addresses, and appointments, but these systems generally are more limited in capacity because they do not interface with a computer. A more advanced style is actually considered to be a **palmtop computer** (also known as a "personal digital assistant"), and this type is much more sophisticated. It operates much like a personal computer, and it can be connected to a fax machine or an online service or linked to your computer for information exchange. Palmtop computers function like organizers, keeping phone numbers and appointments, but they often include word processing and spread sheet capabilities and sometimes wireless faxing and data reception. Keep in mind that the more bells and whistles the unit has, the more likely it is to be somewhat ungainly to carry around with you.

If you're in the market for some type of electronic organizer, here are some points to consider:

- ■ Compare size and weight of the models you're considering.
- ■ Will information be entered by typing onto a keyboard, or writing with a pen onto the screen? If there is a keyboard, check for comfort. If you have large hands, some styles may feel too small. The newest models take commands from handwriting; check for how accurately the style you're considering interprets your handwritten notes.
- ■ Compare screens. Make sure the one you like is easy to read. Ones that are backlit seem to be most adaptable to a variety of conditions.
- ■ Is there a way to back up your data?
- ■ Ask for a demonstration of any of the special features in which you're interested. You want to make certain the "extras" you're looking for are adequate for your needs.

One primary advantage of the palmtop computers over the smaller organizers is the back-up capacity. Because the palmtop can interface with your desktop computer, you can print out information from it and run a full backup of the data as well.

2

GET IT DONE!

WHAT'S AHEAD

The Master List
Creating Your Daily "To Do" List
Don't Forget
Fifteen Easy Tips to Better Manage Your Time
Time-Savers
Time-Wasters

Sometimes the most difficult thing to accomplish at work is work. With telephone calls, meetings, visitors, faxes, and a deluge of mail, it can be almost impossible to get anything done. My clients say, "What can I do?" I tell them to start with a Master List.

THE MASTER LIST

A "running" Master List is the most effective method for keeping track of what needs to be done. It keeps all your "to do" tasks in one place and eliminates all the notes and lists you started, never finished, or can't find.

- First, you need a spiral notebook (lefties may prefer the stenographic style with the spiral on top). Or you may decide to keep your Master List on your computer.

- Write down everything that needs to be done, including tasks related to both long- and short-term goals, and ranging  from the simplest phone call to the first step for a major project. On the left side of the page, note down the date of the entry; on the right side, note the task's deadline.

- A major task should be broken down into parts. If you don't have time to think through all the steps now, leave extra space for writing them down later.

- Set priorities, and put stars next to these items:

    —A task that is essential to you or to the company;

    —A task with a high pay-off;

    —A task that is high priority to your boss;

    —A task that can only be done by you.

- All papers related to projects on your Master List belong in files—not stacked on your desk. (See Chapter 11, "The Desk.")

CREATING YOUR DAILY "TO DO" LIST

- At the end of each day, prepare tomorrow's "to do" list—a list of all the projects to be undertaken the following day. Set aside ten minutes for this task.

- Delegate or carry over any undone tasks from your current "to do" list. Next, review your schedule for the upcoming day, and select the items from your Master List that you can expect to accomplish. If you have a big block of time, select a major project to work on, or if your next day's schedule is broken up by meetings, choose several less demanding tasks that can be slipped into slots during the day. Don't write down more than you think you can accomplish.

- Place a star by the one or two items that are most important. If your day takes an unexpected turn, you'll know what project should take priority during any available time.

- Don't overschedule. Plan no more than 75 percent of the day so you'll have time to cope with interruptions and other unexpected office problems.

- Update your Master List at the end of each day. Cross out the items you have finished (terrific!), and note the date. Write down any new items you think of.

- Keep your Master List notebook for several months:
- It provides a "diary" of sorts. You can look back and confirm: "I did call you—on March 12."
- It helps control procrastination; if an item has been on your Master List for more than a month, you have three options:
  1. Delegate it.
  2. Make time to do it now.
  3. Cross it out. Maybe it wasn't that important.

FIFTEEN EASY TIPS TO BETTER MANAGE YOUR TIME

1. If you don't know where your time goes, keep a log for a week. (See sample Daily Time Log.) As you evaluate the tasks that consumed your time, ask yourself:
   - Did I really need to do this?
   - Could I have delayed this task in order to work on a task of higher priority?
   - Could someone else have done this?
2. Get an early start. If you come in 15–20 minutes earlier than you usually do, you'll find that you'll be off and running before the pace of the office speeds up.

DON'T FORGET!

You can't do it if you don't remember it, so:

Keep pen and paper in logical places: by your bedside, in your car (look for an "autopad" with pencil attached); by all telephones; in your briefcase. Make notes when you think of them and then take time to add them to your Master List at the office (or you'll be left with a dozen scraps of paper).

Leave messages for yourself on voice mail or on your answering machine.

Use sticky-backed notes to leave reminders where you'll see them. If you need to call a client at 2:00 P.M., post a note on the phone while you're making other calls, a sure way to jog your memory.

If your computer has a calendar program with an alarm feature, set meaningful reminders for yourself.

Set aside items you'll need in advance—whether it's papers for a meeting (these should go in a specific file for that purpose) or papers from home (into your briefcase).

To control morning forgetfulness, leave yourself a note on the kitchen counter:

❏ call Ken to confirm breakfast meeting;

❏ take XYZ file;

❏ umbrella!

Need to remember specific points to discuss at an upcoming interview? Write them down! Whether it's questions to ask at your salary review or items to discuss with a subordinate, don't clutter your mind by trying to remember when a good list will do.

3. Do priority work during your "peak performance" time. If you're a morning person, set aside time in the morning; if you come alive after lunch, block out time then.

4. Make appointments with yourself. If you have a big project that you need to start, set aside time for it and write it on your calendar.

5. Estimate how long you need to finish a certain project; it will help you manage your time. (Always anticipate that projects will take longer than expected.)

6. Review tasks to see if there are ways to do them in less time, with fewer steps.

7. Set time limits on projects. Some tasks just aren't worth spending hours on.

8. Vary your pace. No one can function at top speed all day. After a mentally taxing project, turn to something less demanding. Put small, enjoyable jobs in between tough ones.

9. Be decisive, and then implement the decisions you make.

10. Keep small projects handy for idle moments between meetings or while you're on hold.

11. Expect interruptions. They are inevitable. (See Chapter 3, "Interruptions.")

12. Have to work late? Decide exactly what you expect to accomplish. Set a time limit, and work efficiently.

13. Upset by something? Address it if you can or if you need to, or

DAILY TIME LOG

TIME	ACTIVITY	TIME	ACTIVITY
8:00		1:30	
8:15		1:45	
8:30		2:00	
8:45		2:15	
9:00		2:30	
9:15		2:45	
9:30		3:00	
9:45		3:15	
10:00		3:30	
10:15		3:45	
10:30		4:00	
10:45		4:15	
11:00		4:30	
11:15		4:45	
11:30		5:00	
11:45		5:15	
12:00		5:30	
12:15		5:45	
12:30		6:00	
12:45		6:15	
1:00		6:30	
1:15		6:45	

make notes about what you're considering doing. Then try to put it behind you. A low-level task may get you up and going again.

14. Time off actually makes you *more* productive, so don't work half-time when you intend to be relaxing.

15. Give yourself one enjoyable task to look forward to each day.

TIME SAVERS

- Focus on just one thing at a time.

- Call instead of writing, or jot answers to other people's letters directly onto the bottom of the letter you received. Better yet, send a fax. You can fax anything from a quick note to an entire sales strategy and avoid unnecessary phone time while still getting it to the other party fast.

- Keep essentials close at hand to eliminate jumping up and down for items.

- Cluster "like" projects. If you need to meet with several people in the graphics department, each on a separate matter, see if you can do it sequentially.

- If you have recurring paperwork, set a specific time to do it once a week or monthly. (Note it on your calendar.) By making this routine, you'll find that you get it done without thinking about it.

- If you're the boss and reading time is at a premium, here's a solution: Train someone to scan and read for you, delivering to you a final summation of articles and reports.

- Say no. If professional organizations need volunteers and you're overwhelmed, then answer those calls with a negative. Or if the boss has just dropped another "urgent" project on your desk, and you're currently working on the "urgent" project assigned to you yesterday, you've got to ask that the two of you take another look at priorities. You may need to switch tasks for the day, but first, alert him or her to the conflict.

TIME-WASTERS

- Doing more than one thing at a time. The result: many jobs are started, and few are completed.

  Solution: Make a list and set priorities.

- Letting things build up ("I'll do it later . . .").

  Solution: Do as much as you can as it arrives on your desk.

- Getting sidetracked.

  Solution: Stick with the job at hand. Or, if you're interrupted, note down what the next step of your project will be and just keep coming back to it.

- Failure to anticipate.

  Solution: Establish a plan and stick with it!

- Waiting until the last minute.

  Solution: Set up a a schedule with interim deadlines. Careless errors creep in when you're in a last-minute rush.

- Working in clutter.

  Solution: See Chapter 11, "The Desk." If you're working at a messy desk, your eyes wander and you can't fully focus on the work at hand.

- Trying to do too much.

  Solution: Estimate how long something will take and then factor in extra time to give you some margin.

- Interruptions.

  Solution: Take charge of parts of the day and be available for the inevitable interruptions later on (see the following chapter).

- Waiting time.

  Solution: Take along something to do so that you can take control of your time. (In your office, set a good example: If you must keep someone waiting, let that person know approximately how long you'll be.)

- Checking e-mail (or going on-line) constantly

  Solution: E-mail is one of the most efficient ways to communicate; however, like anything else, you must control it— it shouldn't control you. Set a few (two or three) specific times each day to log on and handle your e-mail (or check online). Other times, resist the urge to "see what's new."

3
INTERRUPTIONS

WHAT'S AHEAD

Create Specific Blocks of Interruption-Free Time
What to Do About Drop-in Visitors
What to Do About the Telephone
Limiting Interruptions
What to Do When You Are Interrupted
Who Is Interrupting You?
Do You Interrupt Yourself?

Interruptions are a normal part of doing business, but if your work day becomes one unending series of them, then you need to take decisive steps to regain control. I've worked with countless business people over the years, and I've learned that no matter what your profession, you need to keep the following in mind:

1. There must be some work time each day that is free of interruptions.

2. You must anticipate interruptions in order to:

   —Prevent them

   —Keep the inevitable interruptions to a minimum

   —Shorten those that do occur

CREATE SPECIFIC BLOCKS OF INTERRUPTION-FREE TIME

- Set aside a specific block of time—30 minutes? an hour?—each day to work uninterrupted. If your work requires you to be available for customers, clients, or patients during working hours, you may need to build in your own "quiet" time:

   1. Come in early. You may even have the office to yourself, providing a better work environment.

   2. Use lunchtime as a quiet time. More and more workers are bringing their lunch or ordering in and using this time as an opportunity to work without interruption.

   3. Stay late. This *can* work, but it's the most challenging option of the three. There are more people around late in the day, there are more distractions, and as you get tired, your resolve may weaken. However, if you're a "night owl" and do your best work late in the day, by all means take advantage of the evening hours.

WHAT TO DO ABOUT:
Drop-in Visitors

- Close your door during the hours you've set aside. If you set up a pattern of being unavailable at a certain time, colleagues and staff members will respect that. Later, open your door so that there is a clear signal that you are now available to meet their needs.

- Use a "Do Not Disturb" sign when you really need to get something done.

- Ask your secretary, assistant, or a colleague to run interference for you at certain times of day.

The Telephone

- Don't accept telephone calls during your "quiet" time. Turn on your voice mail or your answering machine, or ask that your secretary or colleague screen your calls:

   — Provide him or her with a list of people who can interrupt you. There are always a few people for whom you want to be available, and if one of them should call, you wouldn't want to miss it.

   — Give the person doing the screening permission to handle what he or she can. Perhaps someone wants an extra brochure, or a telephone number— those items can be taken care of without you. Request that a log of all calls be kept, along with any message or action taken, so that you'll know what has transpired while you've been out of touch.

- Try to utilize the same block of time daily. Routines are easier to follow than trying to "steal" 30 minutes here and there.

- Write your "interruption-free appointment" block of time on the calendar. (This is particularly important if the time you set aside is irregular.)

- Plan your goal for this time in advance. You may need to go through a backlog of mail or papers, or you may be counting on using the time to move forward with a particular project.

- Can't find peace at the office? Try doing the work that requires concentration in another location. Some people like to work at home; others retreat to a conference room or the local library; a few can actually concentrate in the midst of a friendly restaurant or coffee shop.

LIMITING INTERRUPTIONS

Even with the "quiet" time you set aside, you may still feel that you are interrupted more than necessary. Here are some steps to take to limit through-the-day interruptions (even for people—receptionist, customer service representative, manager—whose jobs mean they will inevitably be interrupted).

- If you are within an office, turn your desk so that you don't face the door. You'll find it less distracting as you work, and if people can't catch your eye as they walk past, you'll find they will be less inclined to step in for "just a minute."

- Group interruptions that are within your control.

  —By phone: Let people know when is the best time to reach you, and then try to accept all the calls that come in at that time. All people want to know is how to get hold of you; few will care when.

  —In person: Make an effort to group all scheduled appointments, meeting with people throughout the morning, for example, while leaving your afternoons free for desk work or items that develop. Also: Let people know that you hold "open office," every day between 4:00 and 5:00 P.M., perhaps. If they have a problem, suggest they drop by then.

- Anticipate: If some of the staff are preparing for a big meeting, consider what they might need from you, and ask them to submit their requests in advance. That way, you can prepare at your convenience rather than as a result of a last-minute interruption.

WHAT TO DO
When You Are Interrupted

■ If you're interrupted in the midst of a train of thought, jot down key words before acknowledging the interruption so that you have a reminder of where you were when interrupted.

■ If it's an interruption that will need to be addressed, ask yourself:
— Must this be a priority today, or can it wait?
— If I must do it, can I delay it for an hour or so to a more convenient time?
— What must I cancel or rearrange to fit it in?

■ When people wander into your office and you are busy, remain standing so they are less inclined to sit down.

■ If you have an extra chair in your office where co-workers tend to lounge, remove it.

■ Put your own priorities first. Learn to say: "Could we discuss this later? I have something I've got to get done."

■ Take control by saying: "I'd love to hear about it. Let me finish what I'm doing, and I'll come to your office when I'm through."

■ Don't prolong the interruption. Resist asking how the sales conference went, or about the family vacation. If you're trying to get something done, small talk will just extend the interruption and further reduce your ability to concentrate.

■ Particularly if you've been suffering through several interruptions, it's tempting to quit. Keep going right back to the project on which you were working.

WHO IS INTERRUPTING YOU?

Set aside one week to keep a log of all the things that interrupt you. Note day of week, time, who interrupted you, and for how long.

Interruption	Necessary?	Day/Time	How Long	Solution

- From this information, you may be able to come to several conclusions:

  —You will likely find that most of your interruptions came from the same people. (It's the old 80/20 rule: 80 percent of the problems come from 20 percent of the people.) Are there specific steps you can take to help those people? Can you have them get their answers from someone else? Can you set a specific time for daily or weekly meetings with them so they needn't interrupt you? What about meeting in their office so that you can control the length of the visit?

—If the interruptions follow a pattern (Monday mornings and Friday afternoons, or 3:00–5:00 every day), try scheduling this as "interruption" time. Be available to those who need you and plan to go through the mail or catch up on correspondence if you should have a few minutes to yourself during this time.

—Try to come up with a solution to as many of the interruptions as possible. (If you're the person the new receptionist phones when she doesn't know how to direct a call, see if a company directory—or additional training—won't help make her more self-sufficient.)

—Are the interruptions coming from a specific department (or from home), reflecting that you need to find a way to provide better answers or information to these people? Maybe the employees interrupting you don't understand the task at hand and need more thorough training or better instructions.

—Is it necessary that *you* be interrupted? Perhaps they are simply used to your being available; if you give them more authority over their work (and request that they no longer check with you on all details), you may be able to minimize the number of times you are interrupted.

DO YOU INTERRUPT YOURSELF?

In countless cases, I find that workers are so accustomed to being interrupted—by the phone, by a colleague, by their secretary—that they simply fall into an "interrupting" rhythm, where they hardly know how to sit and do one thing for a prolonged period of time. They become "hoppers." Mr. Jones sits down to write a letter, notices something, and decides to jot out instructions for his assistant, then the phone rings, and Mr. Jones must pull out a file. Once the file is out, he decides to go ahead and work on the items in it. An hour later, the secretary buzzes in that his next appointment is here. An hour has passed: a letter has been started, instructions to the assistant are half-written, a file is out and partially worked on, and now a new person (with papers to leave with Mr. Jones) has entered the office. Too many things are out; nothing is done; and the problem really started when Mr. Jones failed to stick with his original project—writing that letter.

- To break the "interruption" habit, keep the following in mind:
    1. Stick to the job at hand
    2. Remember your priorities
    3. Follow through and meet your goal for the day

IN ADDITION:

- Before any concentrated work session, be sure you have all your tools and materials with you. Jumping up and down for equipment is a classic (and totally preventable) form of self-interrupting.

- A clear desk helps reduce the tendency for self interrupting, because if there is less visual distraction, it makes it easier to focus on your current project.

- Finish the project you're working on before starting another. If you have too many files staring you in the face, it will be more difficult to concentrate on what you need to get done.

  Important!

- Don't misuse your time by initiating an unnecessary phone call, going online, or taking a break.

- Don't procrastinate!

4
PROCRASTINATION

WHAT'S AHEAD

If You Have Poor Work Habits

Catching Up with the Backlog

Establishing New Work Habits

If You're Feeling Overwhelmed . . .

If You're Desperately Seeking Perfection

If You'd Rather Be Doing Something Else

If You Like a Last-Minute "High"

When Those Around You Procrastinate

"Procrastination is the thief of time," wrote Edward Young, an eighteenth-century English poet.

What was true in the eighteenth century is certainly true today.

Procrastination takes energy, and with it, time. Time spent thinking about the task, worrying about delaying the task, wondering when you will finally do the task . . . plus feeling guilty about working on something besides the project on which you're procrastinating. If you could just get *going*, life would be a lot better.

A friend and business executive who recently became motivated to switch jobs confided: "It took me only two months to accomplish what I've been worrying about and procrastinating on for ten years!"

I F YOU HAVE POOR WORK HABITS

Why do people procrastinate? Here are five reasons:

1. **Poor work habits.** Some people procrastinate on everything! They are so far behind that they are sentenced to daily efforts of trying to keep up with yesterday.

2. **They feel overwhelmed.** They may be overwhelmed by a particular project or by their workload in general. Sometimes they're overwhelmed because they don't know how to do it. Or sometimes they feel the job's too much—it's too time-consuming. They are certain the project will take "forever."

3. **They want to do it perfectly.** Some people become so worried about doing a project (or anything they do!) to perfection that they can't get started—or once started, they can't seem to wrap it up.

4. **They'd rather be doing something else.** Sometimes people simply dislike a certain type of work (filling out expense reports, writing up minutes from a meeting, etc.), and so they wait and wait, perhaps hoping one day they'll be in the mood, or just wishing the task would "go away."

5. **They say they work better by waiting until the last minute and producing under pressure.** These people thrive on that "last minute" rush. But then, just when they are finally ready to get started, something else gets in the way—another report that needs to be completed **now** or a son's Little League team qualifies for the finals which are **today**. Sweat turns to stress and stress turns to panic . . . Next deadline, the cycle begins all over again.

There's little room for procrastination in the workplace. Effective people move right in; ineffective ones put things off. So here are ways to establish work habits that permit you to work on today's work today.

CATCHING UP WITH THE BACKLOG

If you're a procrastinator ready to reform, it's likely that you want to put the past behind you. Here's how to select the important from the forgettable and from the "meant to do" items in your past:

• Make a list of all the projects on which you're procrastinating.

Consult past daily "To Do" lists and note which tasks are carried over week after week. These are now the core of your "Procrastination" list.

- Some of these tasks can be crossed off as irrelevant now that so much time has gone by.

- Add the remainder of the items to your Master List (see Chapter 2, "Get It Done!") and draw a box around the lot of them.

- Each day, choose a task to work on (the most unpleasant one?) from the boxed list until you've completed all your "meant to do" items.

- If necessary, give yourself a warmup period before doing a task you've put off: "I'll call that client just as soon as I finish my morning coffee." However, for some people, "morning coffee" can last until lunch. If this is your work style, then you can't afford to wait. Start on your Procrastination list first thing in the morning. Getting something off the list will jump-start your day.

- Give yourself a pat on the back for getting a burdensome task done. For particularly onerous tasks, promise yourself a new paperback or lunch out with a colleague.

ESTABLISHING NEW WORK HABITS

- Handle what you can as soon as it comes up (toss papers you don't need, return phone calls the day they come in), so that you'll have less on which to procrastinate.

- Start your day with the most difficult task or the one you enjoy least. That way all the rest of the day's work seems easy.

- Create time for important projects by coming in early or staying late.

- To get going on a project, select a start-up task. Need to answer some correspondence? Prepare the envelopes or look up the addresses before actually writing the letters.

- If you're excited about something, try to clear time to start right away. Your excitement level will make the job seem easy.

- Start keeping track of how long things take to gain a better understanding of how much time should be allowed for various assignments.

- Select jobs based on time available. If you have a two-hour block of time, undertake something that requires extra time and concentration.

- Use small chunks of time. Most people think a "major" project requires a "major" block of time (which is difficult to come by). By breaking the project down into small parts, you can use the time available—even five to ten minutes can provide enough time to complete one of the project's small steps.

- If you procrastinate on a particular project, such as filing, letter writing, or filling out reports, consider whether the task can be streamlined: Filing can be simplified by putting the backlog of papers in alphabetical order to make it easier to work through the stack; create "form" letters for all standard correspondence; and to simplify filling out reports, if some of the form is the same month after month, you can enter all that information on the form once and make photocopies.

- For a project that takes several sittings, use the end of one work session to prepare for the next one. Your subsequent work period will be even more productive because during the time in between you'll be subconsciously mulling over that next step.

- Expect problems. Don't tell yourself you'll have all next week to work on something, because another priority will come up, a staff person will be sick, or any number of things may interfere with your plans.

- If the question really is *when*, and you know you *have* to do an assignment sometime, then ask yourself if you want to pay the price of a delay (feeling stressed, rushing through the project, and worrying about when you really will do it).

- Consider the consequences. The image of your boss's face when you say you don't have the material may be the motivation you need to get going.

- Keep a list of accomplishments for the week. When you look back at all you've done, it will give you energy to go on.

- Still procrastinating? Ask: What am I avoiding?

- Some people flit from project to project, never quite finishing anything. If you find yourself doing this, consider your priorities, and remember that finishing is the reason you got started.

- Sometimes procrastination is a decision in itself. If you find you're uncharacteristically stalling on something, ask yourself: What's the worst thing that can happen if I don't do it? Could the task remain undone? Could someone else do it for you?

▌F YOU'RE FEELING OVERWHELMED . . .

- The hardest part is getting started. Once you're involved, it won't seem so overwhelming. Here are five ways to get going:

  1. The first step in any project is to break the project down into manageable parts and list those as separate steps. Focus on the specific. Don't write "Do research," when what you really mean is "Call Mr. Smith," "Pick up statistical data from the research department," etc. Each step you write down should be simple and quick.

2. Sometimes you have to start somewhere—anywhere. It may take diving in to figure out what the "real" first step is. You can always change your course of action once you get going.

3 Get the worst part of a project over with by doing it first.

4. Make yourself accountable. Ask a colleague to check with you in 24 or 48 hours to be certain you've gotten the project under way.

5. If you're really stuck, work on the project for only ten minutes on the first day. (Tell yourself you can do anything for ten minutes.) Those few minutes of concentration may unblock you. If not, use the ten-minute system each day until the project is finished or you become motivated to continue on your own.

Once up and going, here are tips to keep that project on target:

- Keep asking: Is this the simplest way to do it? Don't make a project more complicated than it is.

- Delegate. Could someone else do certain phases of a project, with you stepping in as needed? You may be burned out on new ideas, while your assistant has plenty of energy for this undertaking.

Important!

- Set deadlines for interim steps.

IF YOU'RE DESPERATELY SEEKING PERFECTION

- Do you have trouble finishing things? Maybe you're reluctant to take full responsibility, or you're striving too hard for perfection. Don't be so hard on yourself; you'll gain from experience, and there's always the next project.

- Perhaps your plan is too grand. Be realistic about what can be accomplished in the time allotted and what is really necessary. Your time investment should be appropriate to the magnitude of the assignment.

- Is there a shorter way to do it? Will there be negative consequences to scaling down the project?

- Remember, it's important to do a project promptly. Do the best you can in the time allowed . . . which is better than not doing it at all.

IF YOU'D RATHER BE DOING SOMETHING ELSE

Even if you like your job, some tasks just aren't fun. Find a way to make (or get!) the best of it:

- Ask for help. Can a secretary or assistant learn to do the task on which you always procrastinate?

- Try making a boring job (monthly expense report?) more pleasurable by listening to the radio. Or take it home to do during a television program you enjoy but usually don't take time to watch.

- Don't let unpleasant tasks build up. Doing one task you dislike isn't so bad if you know that once you're finished there isn't another similar one waiting for you.

- Put recurring unpleasant tasks on your calendar so that you've set aside time to do them routinely. Habit (and keeping up with the backlog) may make the task more tolerable.

- If the task you'd rather not do is something like returning the call of an irate or generally irritable client and you're the only one who can make the call:

    —Consider the worst thing he or she could say to you, and think how you will handle it. Being prepared will make you feel more in control.

    —Consider the consequences of not calling. How would losing the account affect you and your company? (If the answer is, "Not much," maybe this is a client you can afford to lose.)

    —Make a bargain with yourself: "If I get this call over with today, I won't take any work home with me tonight."

IF YOU LIKE A LAST-MINUTE "HIGH"

Some of my clients assure me that their best work is done at the last minute—even overnight. But people get sick, unexpected events occur, and priorities have to change . . . Waiting until the last minute definitely has its drawbacks. If you've routinely worked this way, it's time to reform:

1. Set interim deadlines on the project and ask a colleague to check on your progress. (Set up a "buddy" system, and let your colleague request a favor in return.)

2. Set your final deadline a couple of days before the actual deadline. This may give you the push that you need to get going.

3. Write out a scenario of what will happen if you continue to delay (or the nightmare you experienced when you procrastinated the last time). Leave this "story" in full view. A glance now and then may be the motivation you need to change.

WHEN THOSE AROUND YOU PROCRASTINATE

When it's your staff:

- Discuss the project with them. Be certain they understand how to break the job down into steps.

- Teach your employees to set interim goals with deadlines.

- You don't want to suffer because they procrastinate, so give them a deadline that's earlier than what you really need.

- Encourage pride of ownership which, in turn, should stimulate active involvement. If they make you look good at a meeting, you might be able to publicly acknowledge their help, or if that isn't appropriate, find another way to show them you appreciate their contribution.

When it's the boss:

- Can you explain why you need things early? Perhaps he or she doesn't understand how this affects you.

- If your boss still doesn't cooperate, try asking for material or information earlier than you really need it. Then, even if the boss is a few days late, you can still get the work done.

- Enlist the aid of the boss's secretary or assistant. Perhaps he or she can get things moving more promptly.

5
THE TELEPHONE

WHAT'S AHEAD

The Organized Phone Call
- Outgoing
- Incoming
- How to End a Call

Message-Taking

Voice Mail

Avoiding Telephone Tag

Telephone Directories

Telephone Time-Savers

"I'm away from my desk right now . . ."

"You've reached the office Smith and Smith. If you know the extension of the party you're calling, dial it now. If you need assistance, press '2' now . . ."

"'Hi! This is Bob. I'm in Oregon for the next few weeks. But this handy machine will be picking up my messages "

"Please leave a message after the long beep, *not* the series of short beeps. . . ."

And if you do get a real live person, the call often goes like this:

"Could you spell your last name. . . . Wait, I didn't get that last part. Did you say 'S' as in 'Sam,' or 'F' as in 'Fred?'"

Sound all too familiar? No one is ever in; everyone's in a meeting; your calls aren't being returned; and so-and-so never got your message to begin with. . . .

Though the telephone is often annoying, it's also a major time-saver. By phone we can accomplish in minutes what would take days, weeks, or months to resolve if communication had to be done in person or by mail.

So dial "O" for "Organization" to make sure your office telephone is a time-saver, not a time-waster.

THE ORGANIZED PHONE CALL: OUTGOING

- Consolidate and prioritize all calls you make. You'll be less in-clined to chat if you're working from a "To Call" list that needs to be completed.

- When you look up a phone number in your directory, make note of that number on your "To Call" list. If you have to call back, you don't have to look up the number again.

- For a lengthy call involving several issues, make notes in advance and have at hand all materials you might need.

- Put a priority on calls that will permit someone else to get started or continue working on a project.

- Establish at the outset how long you can talk: "I've got to go into a meeting in five minutes, but I wanted to check in with you first."

- Get to the point of the call right away: "I have two questions for you regarding the Jones account."

- Bring the other person to the point so that he or she doesn't waste your time: "How can I help you?" calls for a direct response.

- As a call progresses and you get the answers you need, take notes so that you don't forget.

- If you feel you need to take a minute to socialize, do so only after you have finished with business.

- After the call, take any action necessary to complete the details: transfer information to your calendar, add something to the files, put back the materials you had pulled prior to the call, etc.

THE ORGANIZED PHONE CALL: INCOMING

Incoming phone calls must be managed to avoid letting your day become one big interruption. Here's how to take control of your telephone:

- Everyone has to be available for calls at some point, so begin by letting people know the best time to reach you.

- For calls that you *never* want to take (solicitations, etc.), use your secretary or assistant as your first line of defense.

- During time when you need to work uninterrupted, provide your secretary or assistant (or a colleague who is covering for you) with a list of people from whom you will take calls—family member, boss, etc. Add to this standing list the names of any potential callers to whom you need to speak that day—if you've had difficulty reaching someone, you don't want to miss their phone call!

- Ask that your secretary find out what the call is about. Perhaps the call can be redirected, or if it's something simple, let him or her take care of the matter. If you will be handling the call, ask that your secretary pull any files or information you will need.

- Give regular callers the names of people on your staff who can help them when you aren't available.

- Create a list of employees who are working on certain projects to make routing of telephone calls easier and more accurate.

- When transferring a call, tell the caller the name, department, job title, and extension of the person. If the caller is accidentally disconnected, he or she won't need to call *you* back.

Important!

- If you have a new call coming in as you're winding up another, finish up the first call before answering the next.

- If people who are important to you for business reasons constantly complain that they can't get through, explore whether your company might install a "hotline" telephone with a private number to give major clients. The phone should ring on your desk with coverage by a secretary or assistant only when you are on the phone or away from your desk.

CONVERSATION DRAGGING ON? How to End It:

☐ "I don't want to take too much more of your time . . ."

☐ "I know you're busy. I'll call you next week with the report ."

☐ "I'll let you get back to . . . "

☐ "Before we end this conversation . . . "

☐ "I've got to go now, but can we talk about this Friday when I see you?"

☐ "I've got to leave in five minutes. Can you sum up your last points?"

☐ "Just one more thing before we hang up . . . "

MESSAGE TAKING

- Everyone has their own set of VIPs. Create a list of these people, complete with addresses and phone numbers, and the names of their secretaries. Anyone who covers your telephone should have this list, so that an office "temp" won't make a major client spell his name—again, and again.

- If a receptionist, operator, or secretary takes messages for you, he or she should always be aware of where you are and when you'll be back. Nothing is more unprofessional than having someone tell a caller: "I don't know where she is," or, "I have no idea when he'll be back."

- Never let an assistant say, "I'll see if he's in." This makes it seem like you're in to some, out to others.

- Have the person covering your phone provide callers with a recommended time to reach you (between 4:00 and 5:00 P.M., for example). If you have voice mail, you can add this information to your outgoing message. Callbacks and interruptions are reduced because the calls are channeled into a time period best suited to you.

- Remind those who answer your phone to get the caller's name early in the conversation.

- If a caller has to be put on hold, do so briefly and sparingly.

- Tired of reading messages from little scraps of paper? Here are two better ways for your organization to keep track:

1. A running log: Keep a running log of all calls, the numbers, and the reasons for the calls. This provides the person for whom the messages were left with a single list from which to work and makes it easier to set priorities because it's all spelled out on one sheet.

2. A carbonless message book: Use one of the carbonless message books that provides a message slip as well as a permanent record of incoming calls. The slip goes to the person for whom the message is intended; the message book provides a permanent reference for secretary, receptionist, or assistant.

- Most people don't need a record of in-house messages, so a conventional message pad is fine for these calls. Staple together loose messages or use a spindle.

VOICE MAIL

The installation of voice-mail systems throughout the business world offers many time-saving advantages:

- Callers can leave messages 24 hours a day, seven days a week, regardless of time zones. What's more, you can reduce callbacks by leaving a longer, more accurate message than when someone must write everything down.

TIME SAVER

- By giving a single command, users can send the same message to a predetermined group of recipients.

- Messages can be stored and retrieved selectively.

- Messages left for one person can be forwarded to others, saving the time of repeating what was said.

- Message slips are reduced and workers can do other things.

- Unauthorized people can't glance through the messages.

- The systems can combine with beeper/paging systems if appropriate to your business.

To use voice mail effectively:

- Record a short, clear, informational message. You may want to include where you are and when you'll be checking back.

- Change your message for vacations.

- If you will be out of touch for a time, always leave the name of someone else for callers to contact.

- Retrieve your messages frequently.

If a secretary or assistant screens your voice mail, they should:

- Log all the calls that have come in through voice mail.

- Save those that are detailed and might better be listened to by the person to whom the message is directed.

When leaving messages on voice mail:

- Organize your thoughts before calling.

- When you get the company's primary recording, you can usually avoid having to listen to the long list of instructions by pressing "0" or the extension you want right away.

- Always leave your name, phone number, and a good time to reach you so that they can call you back.

- If you are leaving an answer to a question or need an answer, be brief and to the point.

AVOIDING TELEPHONE TAG

- Most executives are only available for telephone calls about 30 percent of the work day, so it's important to figure out how best to reach them.

- When you can, set telephone appointments.

- Call before 9:00 or after 5:00 when they are likely to be answering their own phones.

- Send an e-mail or a fax instead. While the telephone will always be necessary for longer discussions, e-mail is quickly replacing the telephone when the information is short and to the point: "The meeting is scheduled for Monday at 5 P.M." or "I agree with you regarding the XYZ account. Feel free to use my name when you talk to Bob." Frequent e-mail users report tremendous time-savings.

- Befriend secretaries; thank assistants. Make a point of learning the person's name so that you can build a comfortable relationship. It makes him or her more willing to help you get through.

- If an assistant or secretary has been particularly helpful, you might write a personal thank-you note—or tell the boss what a good job he or she is doing.

- When you call back, always mention to the person answering the phone that you're returning a call; it makes you a higher priority to be put through or for the person to call back later.

- If the person you're calling isn't in, and you must leave a message:

  —Give them a time when you'll be available to receive the call.

  —Provide as much information as possible so that the other person is prepared to discuss the topic when you do make contact.

- For the hard-to-reach: Ask for a recommended time to call the person back. Though you'll likely have to fit it in outside your own telephone hour, at least you've pinned down a time.

- Get the name of someone else who might help you. Try to develop second or even third contacts, too.

- If you hit voice mail and wanted to know the person's schedule, try hitting "0" on your touch-tone phone during the message. On many systems, it directs you to the secretary or receptionist who may be able to answer your question.

TELEPHONE DIRECTORIES

- If you use a roll-file for telephone numbers, color code personal and business file cards for easier reference.

- Create cross-references. If you write down John Smith (a computer consultant you just met) under "Smith," you may have forgotten his name when you need help with your computer six months later. You'll be able to find his number if you've also entered his information under "C" for "computer."

- Near the entry for each person, add information that will help you build a personal rapport: The date and occasion of your first contact, who referred you, the association through which you met, spouse's name, and so on.

- You, your assistant, your secretary, and any other staff members should have copies of the company telephone directory to make rerouting calls easier.

TELEPHONE TIME-SAVERS

- A speaker phone can increase your efficiency by freeing both your hands when making short calls or while on hold. A drawback is that for prolonged calls, the person at the other end is often bothered by the barrel-like sound quality; it's also not appropriate for private conversations.

- For those (including executives) who spend long periods on the telephone, a headset can be an asset. Sound quality is good and privacy is automatic. In addition, neck and back strain are relieved by not having to cradle the receiver on your shoulder during lengthy calls while you're likely trying to handle papers at the same time.

- Have a clock visible. It will remind you of the time.

- If you're really trying to shorten calls, purchase an inexpensive timer. Estimate how long you're willing to spend on a given call, and set the timer. When the bell rings, you'll know it's time to close the conversation.

- Periodically, evaluate your phone usage. Create a log on which you note telephone calls, their length, and the nature of the call. At the end of the week, evaluate which calls were necessary which might have been delegated, and which were simply wasted time.

WORTH THE TIME

TELEPHONE LOG

Caller	Subject	Call initiated by	Length

- Use airport time or time spent waiting for a table at a restaurant to get necessary phoning done.
- Save time by communicating in writing. A memo with a reply form at the bottom will indicate that the person needn't call back with a reply.

- Save time by using the telephone:

—Always confirm appointments. There's usually no change, but you'll save time if someone "forgot" to cancel. (When you make an appointment, note the phone number by the appointment to save having to look it up.) When you confirm, ask travel and parking directions if you've never been there before.

—When possible, schedule meetings by telephone. By setting up a conference call, you can save yourself a trip across town, across the country, or down the stairs to another department within your company.

Remember to:

1. Schedule a conference call just as you would a meeting.

2. Notify people of the meeting and fax or mail them an agenda so that they are prepared.

PART TWO

PAPER

MANAGEMENT

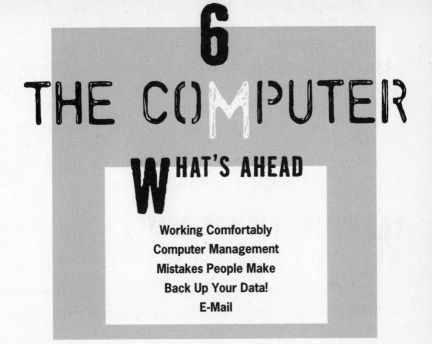

6
THE COMPUTER

WHAT'S AHEAD

Working Comfortably
Computer Management
Mistakes People Make
Back Up Your Data!
E-Mail

Only a modern-day Rip Van Winkle would think that he can survive in the business world without making use of a computer.

Today the computer is a vital management tool whereby staff and bosses alike can save time and work smarter because of the incredible possibilities brought to them via the latest technology: Companies can now operate more efficiently using computers to reduce drudgery; they can conduct computer research in international databases, chart sales, and keep detailed track of clients as well as the competition. Institutions are finding that desktop publishing is cheap and fast, and when instruction manuals are kept permanently on the computer, it reduces printing costs and the manuals can be kept totally current. And surely you've met the executives who "can't live" without their electronic mail or portable computer "notebooks"?

While the vast numbers of businesses and the various types of computers prevent me from offering specific prescriptions as to how best to "organize" your computer, what I can do is offer some guidelines that will help you stay on top of whatever system you use.

WORKING COMFORTABLY

As office workers are spending more and more time at their computers, it's important the set-up be arranged to prevent strain and provide maximum comfort:

- Your keyboard should be at elbow level so that your hands rest on it comfortably. If the table on which the computer sits is a little high, consider a keyboard extender. These attach underneath the computer table and pull out at a more convenient level.

- The top of the computer screen should be at eye level or slightly below so that your eyes focus down slightly as you work.

- Many offices are overlit, and the area around your computer may be too bright. Visors for the computer or antiglare filters that attach to the screen (available through computer supply companies) can help.

- Avoid long, uninterrupted stints (more than an hour) at the computer. Find a good stopping place, walk down the hall, stretch, or spend a few minutes at another activity.

COMPUTER MANAGEMENT

Computer files are out of sight, but they shouldn't be out of mind. Like any file system, they've got to be kept up to date and well maintained.

- If you're not yet that comfortable with your computer, ask the person who installs the system or an expert within the company to help you set up your system. You should have easy access to a "menu" screen from which you can choose the program you intend to use.

- You'll also want a well-thought-out system for managing your files. IBM and compatibles use subdirectories; the Macintosh uses folders. Computer manuals often use the analogy of a tree: your subdirectories are the branches, and each should consist of a separate, logical category of work.

- A good way to manage various projects is to establish a general directory (or folder on the Macintosh) for each facet of your work.

Within that directory, create a subdirectory or file (if the category isn't extensive) for each client, project, or piece of correspondence.

- As with paper files, be consistent in your file names. A well-named file will tell you the client or project, the type of file (correspondence? invoice?), and if it's one of several drafts, then a number will indicate which one. The second draft of an article for a business journal might be in a "writing" directory, and the file itself might be labeled "nybiz2.art," shorthand for "New York business article, 2nd draft." Macintosh files can be labeled less cryptically.

- When a directory or a folder contains more than a screen's worth of files, it's time to create a new directory.

- If you've lost track of how and where you've filed certain data, there are search programs available that will go through your database for key words to help you locate a missing file.

- Even though you can't see your hard disk, it needs to be "organized" so that you gain maximum capacity and maximum speed from it. Ask about an optimization program that can "tidy up" your disk so that the data is stored in the most efficient way.

- Clean out your files regularly—and yes, I mean your computer  files! Delete duplicate files and anything that you'll never need again. Transfer to disk inactive files that are not presently needed.

- Use color coding on the disks you use for inactive projects and for back-up. If your paper filing system is color-coded, use the same code for your disks: accounting information on green; customer list on blue; and so on.

- Label your disks, and keep a paper print-out of the directory so that you'll have a quick reference sheet telling you exactly what is on each disk.

- Keep disks protected by storing them in the specially designed storage cases, and remember that light, heat, dust, and any type of magnetization can be damaging.

- Information on disks can fade over time. If you keep data for more than twelve months, copy it annually so that you're never storing data on the same disk for more than a year.

MISTAKES PEOPLE MAKE

- **Not learning the operating system (usually DOS).** If you "only use the computer for word processing" or for "the accounting program," you're not taking full advantage of your computer. Being able to maneuver through the underlying system is a skill that can be enormously beneficial, particularly with all the coming office technology.

- **Letting the "computer person" set up everything.** While I'm the first to recommend calling in an expert, you need to be there to advise so that the system is well organized for you (there are a good number of organizational decisions made during the set-up, such as the initial basis for your tree and its branches). If you're involved, you'll be certain the system is right for you, and what's more, you may learn something!

- **Not reading the manual or using the tutorial** (or dozing through the mandatory computer class your company made you take). The class or the tutorial may be a little boring, but the knowledge will save you a lot of time in the long run. If the manual isn't "user friendly," stop by your local bookstore. Chances are someone has written a guide to the software program that you can understand.

- **Not using the support numbers for help.** Whether it's an internal department or the support service run by the software manufacturer, you'd be amazed what these wizards can do for you by phone. I've heard of them helping with everything from teaching someone how to turn on their system to unjamming a printer to saving a document the user was *certain* he'd accidentally lost.

- **Not keeping up to date.** The first step is as easy as filling out the postcard that comes within any computer program you buy. The company will make you aware of updates. If you have a specific complaint, call and tell them what you want corrected. They're looking for feedback, and with luck, your improvement will be on the updated program. For more general information on the computer industry and what's coming up, go to a newsstand and buy the four or five computer magazines that are being published today. A glance through them will tell you which one is best for you.

- **Tampering with the originals.** If you use boilerplate information (text repeated in all pitch letters, invoices, contracts, etc.), create originals and use them for file reference only. When you need to create a new document, copy the information and edit only from the copy so that your original will be intact next time you need it.

- **Not backing up the data.** Make copies of everything. I know—you never photocopied all your paper files, but your risks were less then. There's no bigger time-waster than having to reenter information lost through a power surge or a drive breakdown.

BACK UP YOUR DATA!

■ Purchase a backup program or request that your computer consultant create a macro so that backing up your material is as simple as entering a few commands. When purchasing a program, consider:

—Is it fast and easy to use?

—Do you have to be there during the backup?

—Will the system easily hold the amount of information you'll be backing up?

- Develop a routine schedule for backing up your computer files. That way you won't forget.
- You'll need enough backup disks or tapes to have a different one for each day of the week as well as for a monthly copy.
- Create at least three levels of backup:

  —a monthly backup, which should be a total backup of your entire hard drive to be saved until the end of the next month. This backup can be a lifesaver if your computer has picked up a bug you don't discover for a few days. (This means your weekly and daily backups may be infected.) By creating this piece of "ancient history," you'll have a way of recreating your data minus the bug.

  —a weekly backup, which should also be a full backup (your Friday backup copy, saved until the following Friday).

  —a nightly backup. This can be selective—only the vital work of the day, or a total backup if you prefer.

- At least one current copy of your backup, probably your monthly copy, should be kept off premises. However, if you've been working on something important, drop your daily backup in your briefcase every night, and leave the previous night's backup at the office.
- If it's very important, create two copies. Many companies routinely run two copies of their database nightly; one stays on the premises, the other goes home with an employee.

E-MAIL MANAGEMENT

E-mail is an easy, fast way to correspond. Once you begin using it, you'll find that a 20-second e-mail can quickly replace a 10-minute phone call.

- Establish specific times to answer your e-mail, just as you should with your regular mail. It's more efficient for you, and your e-mail correspondents will become familiar with your schedule and will learn to expect to hear from you first thing in the morning (or whatever schedule you set for yourself).

- Scan the incoming messages by order of importance, using the sender or the subject line to make a judgment. If you're running low on time and have not answered all your messages, skim through the remaining list, and do one of three things:

  1. Answer the more important immediately;

  2. Save the significant for the next day;

  3. Delete everything else so you don't waste time on it the next time you log on.

- Keep your own messages clear and to the point. Be specific about what you need to know so that the message you get in return will also be concise.

- Enter e-mail addresses in your personal address book as well as your online one.

- Try to handle your e-mail while you're out of town. Whether this means traveling with a laptop or logging on from a computer in an office you're visiting, it's worth the effort. You can dust off a good number of problems by checking in regularly, and it will prevent you from returning to a long backlog of e-mail.

Junk mail exists in e-mail form, too. Here's how to stay off the lists:

- **Be cautious about giving out your name and e-mail address if you want to limit who you hear from.**

- **Check out special mail preference services through online services and the Internet to specify that you don't want to be on general mailing lists.**

- **If you receive unwanted e-mail, notify the sender. They are supposed to remove you from their lists.**

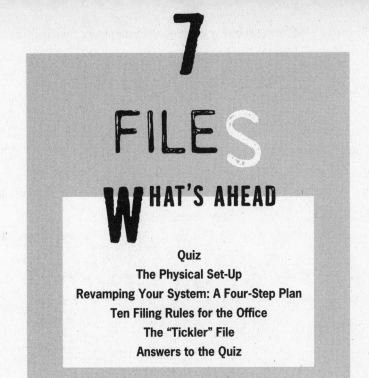

7
FILES

WHAT'S AHEAD

Quiz
The Physical Set-Up
Revamping Your System: A Four-Step Plan
Ten Filing Rules for the Office
The "Tickler" File
Answers to the Quiz

I recently visited the office of a top cosmetics executive and learned of an innovative filing system: Every piece of paper, every reference book, and every file was left out.

"I'm afraid if I put it away, I'll never find it again," explained the executive. "This way I know where everything is."

"There's only one problem," I answered, after scanning the room. "There's no place to sit down!"

If you're wondering about your filing system, please take this quiz:

QUIZ: PART ONE

If your answer is yes to any of the questions below, put a check in the box:

- ❏ Do you put papers in temporary parking places?
- ❏ Do you ever keep papers "just in case . . ."?
- ❏ Do you frequently have to sift through stacks of paper, searching for something?
- ❏ Would it take you longer than 30 minutes to catch up with your filing?
- ❏ Are your file drawers stuffed?

QUIZ: PART TWO

WHAT WOULD YOU DO WITH:

1. A business magazine you need to read.
2. Research material a subordinate has just given you that you need for a report.
3. A written request from someone for some information.
4. A booklet explaining new company benefits.
5. A memo requesting your presence at an upcoming staff meeting.

If you checked off even a few of the questions in Part One and think that you might have simply "piled" any of the items in Part Two of the quiz, then this section will take the chaos out of your office files.

(See the end of the Section [p. 83] for the correct answers to Part Two)

THE PHYSICAL SET-UP

Most employees use the company's existing file system, but if you *were* to have a choice, here are some elements to keep in mind:

- Encourage the company to spend what is needed for top-quality file cabinets; they should last for years. Inexpensive systems are difficult to manage and awkward to open and close. When it comes to cabinet style, consider:

  1. Vertical file cabinets: These offer the maximum file storage in the least amount of space. Choose from styles that hold legal- or regular-size documents.

  2. Lateral file cabinets: These open to the side and offer handy desk-side file storage. They are particularly convenient because no file is really at the back the way they are in a vertical unit. A two-drawer size also can double as a credenza or a room divider. A disadvantage is that in tight spaces (such as filing rooms), the side opening feature can create traffic problems.

  3. Open lateral files: With this system, files are slipped into place from the side, and filing is done quickly because there are no drawers to open and shut. (Ideal for anyone doing a lot of filing.) Because they are less attractive and the files can collect dust, these are best used in company file rooms—traffic is low and the open files are not on public view.

- Also consider whether or not your company needs burglar- or fire-proof units.

- Whichever cabinet style you select for your own office, you will find your files more accessible with a suspension filing system ("hanging" files that hold regular file folders). Filing and retrieval are simplified, and the suspension files prevent the "domino" effect within a drawer.

REVAMPING YOUR SYSTEM: A FOUR-STEP PLAN

If the time has come to clean up your files, then you'll need the following:

- **New file folders.** Don't start a new system with torn-up file folders. They won't last. Buy one-third or one-fifth cut folders for better visibility, and if you are using suspension files, ask for the folder style designed to be used with this system (they are lower cut)

- **Suspension files to hold the file folders.** Those with square-cut bottoms offer added accessibility because the files aren't all being squeezed into a V-shaped bottom

- **Plastic tabs and insert labels** for the suspension files

- **File labels** (in several colors)

- You'll also need:

  —Pen

  —Cardboard boxes (for holding the papers until you sort them into files)

- Set aside time for this project. You'll need a couple of hours for your first session. Once you've got a system, you may be able to use an assistant to get all the files in order.

STEP ONE:

- First, go through your existing files one by one, and consider the value of maintaining each one:

  —Is this file still relevant?

  —Can it be tossed?

  —Should it be with active files in my area?

  —Should it go to "dead" storage? "Dead" storage may be boxes in the company's basement or file cabinets in a warehouse several miles from your office. Items placed here are ones that you will likely not need but must maintain for legal or business reasons.

STEP TWO:

- Next, go through any unfiled papers and put them through the following test:

  —Will I ever need this again? If I do, is there another easy way to get it (company library, computer reference, etc.)? (If there is, you needn't file it.)

—Does this add anything new to what I already have on the topic?

—When and how will I want to retrieve it? This decision will help you select the appropriate file and category. New industry data might go in "Annual Sales Meeting" or in "Marketing" files, depending on how you intend to use it.

- Put aside papers you can't categorize. By the end, you may find that several items fall into a logical grouping.

- Unfold letters before filing.

- Whether you can finish in one session or whether it takes several, just keep working until you have everything filed.

- Once you have developed new work habits you will learn to purge files frequently, whenever you happen to have the file out. This reduces a future need to set aside special time to clean out your files.

TIME SAVER

STEP THREE:

- Create categories. Now that you have an overview of your files, decide upon the major groupings into which you want to put them: "Clients," "Suppliers," etc. Major categories, such as "Clients," may command an entire drawer with subcategories within, such as "Clients—International" and "Clients—Domestic."

- Titles of categories and of the files themselves should always begin with a noun. You'll think of "Expansion" plans before you think of "Revised Expansion" plans.

- Categories should be placed in alphabetical order, and files within categories should be put away alphabetically (or chronologically, if that is more significant).

- As you create these categories, you'll also need to decide where the category itself belongs:

  —If you use files in this group weekly, keep them in a file cabinet near you.

  —Monthly? Keep the files within your department, but perhaps out near your assistant or secretary.

  —Every two to three months? These files can be placed in a company file room.

STEP FOUR:

- Write or type labels CLEARLY. Surprisingly, handwriting can sometimes make for a more accessible system since the typewritten letters give a similar overall appearance.

- Color coding can work wonders. Many offices color-code by subject. However, businesses that file by client or patient names (medical offices) can color-code by letter of the alphabet. (A = red, B = blue, etc. Start over when you run out of colors.) For letters such as "S" that have so many names, split the letter into two colors: one for "SA–SK" and another for "SL–SZ."

- For documents that for legal or financial reasons must not be lost or misplaced, use file folders with two-punch fasteners at the top. Place the most recent paper on top. Filing within these folders takes extra time, so use these only when absolutely necessary.

- Some files—particularly those used by several people—may require "histories." For example, a file on a new prospect to whom your company is trying to make a sale should have details of each conversation so that no matter when or why the prospect is called, members of your company know and understand the history of the relationship.

- Create an index for bulky files, and keep it in the front of the file. This index should list the material in order of placement within the file.

- Keep a master list of all files that have been created. Store this list in a notebook kept on top of the file cabinet or on a piece of paper in front of the first file in the top drawer. One person should be in charge of adding or deleting as things change.

- Leave 3–4 inches of extra space in file drawers to avoid overstuffing.

- If your company has a file room and staff, there should be a system for returning files:

  1. Each person should have a "Return to File" tray in their office from which the file person can collect material daily. Or:

2. Each person should be responsible for dropping off the files used that day in the file room. Designate a tray for that purpose.

- If you need to file back issues of magazines, store the magazines themselves in magazine file boxes available from office supply stores. Label the file boxes as to magazine and date, and file them chronologically.

WORTH THE TIME

1. Purchase a looseleaf binder and some plastic-sleeved pages.

2. From each magazine to be saved, photocopy the table of contents. Place them in chronological order within the plastic-sleeved pages of the looseleaf binder.

3. To locate an article, you can skim through the binder and quickly find the article—and the issue—you need.

- Remember that not everything belongs in a traditional file:

—Businesses that require vast amounts of documentation (law firms, for example) generally put files on microfilm.

—Sometimes a notebook is a handier reference. If you want a secretary to have sample letters of a certain type to refer to, then create a notebook that holds letters that have been sent out in the past.

TEN FILING RULES FOR THE OFFICE

1. Every paper that comes across your desk that will need to be filed should have the following information noted on it:

   —date and source

   —the file in which it should be placed; note this on first reading so that you won't have to reevaluate the information later

   —a "Destroy after_____" (date), if possible; this will make it easier to clean out the file in the future

2. File regularly (or be sure your staff does). Some people file a piece of paper as they finish with it (the fastest way to get it done). Others place a "To File" tray on their desk to collect items and then file at the end of the day.

3. Every time you start a new project, create a file folder for it. This is far more efficient than stacking the information somewhere.

4. If a piece of paper would be appropriate in two separate files, photocopy the item and put it in both, or place a cross-referencing note in one file and the article in the other file.

5. Staple relevant material together. Paperclips tend to catch on other papers within the file.

6. Organize within the file. If dates are particularly relevant, order chronologically. If there are several names included in one file, then organize alphabetically.

7. If you have to take something out of a file for any length of time, leave a note, specifying the item's whereabouts. If the files are used by several people, create "flags" (a colored piece of paper with the person's name on it) that are left on top of the file cabinet until needed. If an entire file is removed, a flag should be placed where the file was removed so that it is clearly visible to anyone opening the file drawer. By having a "readymade" system, people are more likely to comply.

8. Weed out regularly. Whenever you pull a file, take a few minutes to toss what is no longer relevant. On the inside of the file folder, note the date on which you last sorted through it so that you have a record of how long it's been since the file was purged.

9. Any file more than 2 inches thick should be removed and sorted through.

10. If you're no longer referring to certain files, they should be reevaluated. Should the information be tossed, moved to a different section of the company's files, or should it be placed in "dead" storage?

THE "TICKLER" FILE

A "Tickler" file system is the key to managing those "pending" papers—papers you'll need "soon," but not quite yet:

- You'll need a folder for all 12 months for long-range items, and folders for each day of the month (30–31) for short-range items, so set aside 43 folders for this new system. Label 12 of them by month. On the remainder, put only numbers: "1," "2," . . . through to "31."

- **To use:** If it's September 5, and you want to date-file a letter that requires follow-up on September 22, place the letter in the folder marked "22." If you plan to follow up in October, the letter should be placed in the "October" file. On October 1, pull the "October" file, sort through it, and place all the papers into files that correspond with the appropriate dates.

- These are your "action" and "reminder" files. Each day—and at the beginning of each month—this file will hold backup materials for the items you want to be reminded to do at that time.

ANSWERS TO
THE QUIZ: PART TWO

1. The business magazine could be processed in one of two ways:

   —If you have a set time for business reading (during commuting time? at home at night?), place the magazine directly into your briefcase.

   —Otherwise, take a moment to scan the articles and rip out those you'll read. File them in your "Reading" file.

2. The research material you need for your report should go into a labeled file folder created to hold all the information pertaining to your report. Then, when you're ready to work on it, everything you need is in one place.

3. A letter requesting information should be delegated or processed as quickly as possible. If you absolutely can't do it today, place the letter in your "Tickler" file for the next day. After sending the information, toss the letter, or if you need to document that it was answered, note the date it was mailed and file the letter with similar correspondence.

4. The company benefits book should be scanned for anything you need to know now; then file it in your "Benefits" or "Employment" file. While you have that file out, take a moment to skim through it and pull information that is out of date.

5. Note the information on your calendar, and toss the memo.

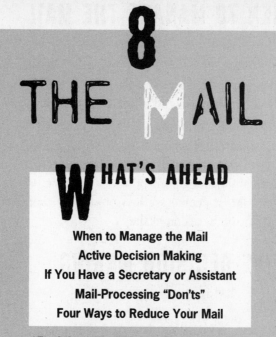

8
THE MAIL

WHAT'S AHEAD

When to Manage the Mail
Active Decision Making
If You Have a Secretary or Assistant
Mail-Processing "Don'ts"
Four Ways to Reduce Your Mail

For information on e-mail, see page 69.

The mail! More mail? Like it or not, there's no stopping it. Through rain, sleet, snow, and even disorganized mailrooms, the mail is going to get through to your office—and if you don't process it efficiently, it's going to create an ever-increasing amount of clutter.

If you can master the daily mail—processing all of it every day—you will instantly gain extra time; no more rereading, no more mail shuffling, no more wondering "where did I put that . . . ?"

WHEN TO MANAGE THE MAIL

- Whether your office receives one mail delivery or more, secretaries and assistants should process the mail as soon as it arrives so that anything urgent can be spotted immediately.

- If your assistant has scanned for anything urgent, then you may prefer to manage the mail mid- or late morning to preserve the first block of time for getting priority work done. Or wait until late afternoon. Most people are less productive then, yet mail processing can still be accomplished.

ACTIVE DECISION MAKING

- Process each incoming piece of mail as quickly as you can. Here are the choices:

    1. Toss. Much of your mail can go into the wastebasket. Throw out unsolicited sales literature, dispose of thank-you-for-seeing-me notes from salespeople; even a reminder note for a meeting or a dentist appointment should be thrown out just as soon as you've noted the time and the place in your calendar.

    2. Forward to someone else. Maybe you've received a letter that should be handled by another department, or perhaps it could be delegated to a staff member. Bills to be paid should be approved and sent on to accounting. Get it off your desk as fast as you can!

3. Act on it. Can you answer with a quick phone call? Or how about jotting a reply to someone on the bottom of the letter and simply sending it right back, keeping a copy for your records if need be? You can even write out or dictate a reply to be formally typed. Delaying your response will mean rereading the letter and deciding again what it was you wanted to say—a major time-waster.

4. File. The agenda for next month's committee meeting should be skimmed and dropped into the "Upcoming Meeting" file. The report you requested on a new product should go directly into the appropriate file. If your files are convenient, and it's only an item or two, file those papers immediately. Otherwise, create a "To File" folder or use a paper tray, and slip it in there for you or your assistant to file later.

5. Place on temporary "hold." Some projects just can't—and shouldn't—be fully acted upon when you process the mail. There are three ways to handle "hold" items:

a. Put items you need within a day or two in a "To Do" file that you go through daily. Also note the related task in your spiral notebook (or computer) where you keep your Master List (see Chapter 2, "Get It Done!"). If possible, choose a block of time when you expect to get around to working on the project and note it on your calendar.

b. Sometimes you need to defer making a decision: You'd like to attend a reception to which you received an invitation—but you can't decide until your upcoming business trip plans are confirmed. It's fine to defer the decision, but you must decide *when* you will decide. Select the time when you will be able to commit, and date-file the relevant material in the appropriate "Tickler" file. (See Chapter 7, "Files.")

c. Some businesses have a permanent "hold" file for material that must be retained until it is replaced. Weekly pricing schedules are a good example of incoming mail that will be filed only until the next list arrives in a week.

6. Read. If a piece of mail will take less than five minutes to read or scan, do it now., Other items should be placed in a "To Read" file, or if it's a trade publication you always go through on your commute home, put it directly into your briefcase.

IF YOU HAVE A SECRETARY OR ASSISTANT

The volume of mail most business people receive is astounding, and if your secretary/assistant learns to relieve you of some of this daily burden, you will find time you never thought could be available to you:

- A secretary or assistant should be assigned to physically open all the mail. You've already saved time if you don't have to wrestle open an Express Mail box or a plasticized envelope.

- Spend time training a new person to more fully process the mail. For one to two weeks, sort the mail together, explaining why certain procedures are followed.

- Several file folders should be created to ease the passing of mail between secretary and boss. The categories I most often recommend include:

Urgent—for anything that should be looked at immediately

To Do—this would include letters requiring answers; interoffice memos requiring planning, etc.

To Approve—invoices, staff expense reports

To Sign—this folder will hold the letters dictated— and to be signed—as a result of the previous day's mail. Any items for discussion should be so marked—use a sticky-backed flag and make notes.

To Read—journals, magazines, material for meetings, etc.

To File—items that should be saved for reference (the secretary will do this after the boss's "okay")

To Toss?—maintain a file for these items for a few weeks after the initial training sessions. This lets you skim through what your assistant has determined is "junk." After you have confidence in the decisions being made, dispense with this folder.

- Color-code the folders for added clarity. Red for Urgent, etc.

- To the front of each file with more than one or two items, an assistant or secretary should add a list of the contents with any deadlines so that the executive can see at a glance what's inside and when it is due.

- For each incoming item, teach your assistant to ask: Is background information needed in order to respond to this? If an incoming letter is a reply to a letter sent by you, your secretary should pull and attach your letter so that you know the details of the issue in question.

SMART TIP

- After reading through all the mail, it is your job to return to your assistant all the information given to you with notes attached. All items should be kept in the same folder in which they were presented, with very few papers from the day's mail remaining in your office.

MAIL-PROCESSING "DON'TS"

- ■ **Don't** use your "in" box as a holding pen for the incoming mail you're not in the mood to deal with.
- ■ **Don't** create more work for your secretary by disorganizing the papers he or she has organized for you—an office time-waster.
- ■ **Don't** get discouraged because you have a day when the mail gets the best of you. Processing the mail takes practice.

FOUR WAYS TO REDUCE YOUR MAIL

1. Cancel any unnecessary subscriptions.
2. Write to the Mail Preference Service, Direct Marketing Association, P.O. Box 9008, Farmingdale, NY 11735-9008, and ask to be removed from their mailing lists. Provide them with the variations of your name under which you are receiving mail. Your name will be put on a Mail Preference Service List which is circulated among national direct-mail companies, who are then supposed to delete the name from their lists.
3. Create a form letter and write directly to companies requesting that your name be removed from their mailing lists.
4. Drop out of any organizations that are no longer relevant to your professional growth.

PART THREE

WORKING

WITH

OTHERS

9

DELEGATING

WHAT'S AHEAD

Step One: Select What Is to Be Delegated
Step Two: Training
Step Three: Put It in Writing
Step Four: Observe
Step Five: Enjoy and Congratulate
When You've Received an Assignment
When Multiple Bosses Delegate to One Secretary

Smart business people think of delegating as a way to free their own time, but they also know it's important for other reasons: By getting co-workers involved, a stronger team is created.

Delegating is one of the best secrets to getting a job done well and on time.

STEP ONE: SELECT WHAT IS TO BE DELEGATED

- Consider your daily workload and which jobs might be delegated. If no assignments come to mind, then spend a few days keeping a running log of the work you do. This will give you a list to scan for tasks to delegate.

- While some boring tasks must always be delegated, also make an effort to delegate more challenging work. The people around you need to be stimulated and have their capabilities tested.

- Select the person to whom the job should be delegated. Ask yourself, Who is the best person to handle this task? Try to  match the skills required with a qualified employee.

- Sometimes the correct choice is to delegate to an outside service. Companies are now hiring everything from messengers to lawyer-temps to help out on an as-needed basis. If your staff is overburdened or not equipped to handle the task, where can you turn to get the job done?

- Choose the right opportunity for delegating a job for the first time. There should be enough slack in the schedule so that if something goes wrong, there's time to make a correction. The object of delegation is long-term productivity, not just short-term job relief.

STEP TWO: TRAINING

- Set aside uninterrupted time to explain the job.

- Explain what you want accomplished (update mailing list, gather resource material for a report), and discuss how best to do this. Once the person is trained, you will also give a firm date for a progress report.

- Don't assume the person knows how to do something or where certain information is to be found.

- With most assignments, you will want to work alongside the person the first time, making suggestions as he or she goes along.

STEP THREE: PUT IT IN WRITING

- Any project should have an assignment sheet. Devote a different sheet for each project.

- Record:

    —Date assignment was made

    —To whom it was assigned

    —Description of the assignment

    —Due date

    —Any notes

- If you are delegating a project with many parts, assign the tasks so that they will be completed in the correct order and on schedule.

- Checkpoints should be established at the outset so that the person knows in advance that you will need to see the project at various stages. The newer the employee, the more frequent the checkpoints.

DELEGATION SHEET

Date	Name	Assignment	Due Date

Notes:

STEP FOUR: OBSERVE

- As you prepare to give the person some independence, think through the delegated project and anticipate what the employee may need. It's best if you can anticipate the task requirements (special permission to access files, authority to hire temporary help), so that they needn't check back with you for the basics.

- Set a firm completion date. "As soon as possible . . ." is a good way for the project to be put on the back burner. If you need it Friday, say so!

- Let the person know you're available if there are questions.

- Make it clear that you would rather know sooner—not later—if he or she has run into difficulties.

- Don't hover. And let the person make as many decisions as possible. That's why you delegated the job.

- When something goes wrong, don't snatch away the project. Work with the employee to come up with a way to solve the problem.

STEP FIVE: ENJOY AND CONGRATULATE

- At this point, the other person should have the job under control. Your primary task now is to express your appreciation so that they'll feel rewarded for a job well done.

WHEN YOU'VE RECEIVED AN ASSIGNMENT

■ If your boss does a poor job of training and delegating, there are steps you can take to be certain that you do a good job. Know the answers to the following:

1. Understand the assignment. Exactly what is expected?

2. What is the deadline?

3. Is there a budget?

4. Are other people involved?

5. How much authority do you have?

6. Should you check in? When and how often?

■ Even if your boss doesn't think of it, assign yourself interim deadlines. For your own checkpoint system, put these dates on your calendar or in your "Tickler" file.

■ Running into trouble? Sound an alarm earlier rather than later. Sometimes people wait until the last minute to say they have a problem, and by that time, it's too late.

WHEN MULTIPLE BOSSES DELEGATE TO ONE SECRETARY

- Have a group meeting as needed to discuss the workload and to make any office adjustments.

- Use a slotted, labeled telephone message holder to keep track of messages for several individuals.

- Color-coding is vital for keeping everything straight. Assign a color to each boss so that mail, letters to sign, etc., can be placed in appropriately colored folders.

- The secretary's desk should have one "in" basket (for work to be done) and "out" baskets for each boss. Stacking trays are ideal because they take up the least space.

- Work should be processed in the order received.

- Each boss should use flags to denote work that should take priority. If an executive needs something to be done immediately, he or she should be the one to clear it with those who use the same secretary.

- Try to avoid end-of-the-day emergency assignments.

- A secretary should never be used for personal errands. Look for other ways to get these done. (Use a messenger service to pick up theater tickets; hire a teen for home-related errands; etc.)

10

THE ORGANIZED MEETING

WHAT'S AHEAD

Planning a Meeting
Setting Up the Agenda
Running an Efficient Meeting
Attending a Meeting
Ending the One-on-One Meeting

Meetings—you can't live with them (poorly run ones are terrible time-wasters!), but you can't live without them either. Meetings are important for the sharing of information, problem solving, group analysis, and decision making, and for gaining a better understanding of the people with whom you work.

Yet meetings are expensive! Multiply the estimated hourly rate of those attending times the number of hours the meeting will take, and anyone can see that these are costly get-togethers. To be worthwhile, meetings need to be held for a specific purpose and planned with a goal in mind.

Planning a Meeting

- Regular staff meetings are an important part of departmental communication. They should be held at least once a week.

- A manager and an assistant or secretary need to meet daily. Try five-minute meetings; hold them standing up so they don't drag on.

SMART TIP

- Review periodically whether or not internal company committees can be disbanded. You may have work groups that have outlasted their need; meeting time can be saved by dismantling the committees.

- Before scheduling any other type of meeting, ask:

  —Is this meeting really necessary? What will happen if it's never held?

—Would a phone call, a conference call, or a one-on-one meeting be as effective?

—What is the cost of getting together? Is someone leaving an activity even more beneficial to the company in order to attend?

—Is the meeting strictly informational—no feedback necessary? Written communications should be used for most announcements.

- If you decide a meeting is necessary, ask:

—What are we trying to accomplish? (If you can't state a goal, you're not ready for a meeting.)

—Who should come to help achieve the goal?

- Invite only those who are needed, but be certain that you've included people who may be important later on. (Sometimes the people who will implement a new strategy are left out of planning meetings, yet they can give valuable opinions on a new idea's viability.)

- A limited invitation list makes for the most efficient meeting. However, the group can still benefit from the input of others:

—Solicit information from some people in writing instead of requesting that they attend in person.

—Schedule the meeting so that certain people attend for specific periods of time, keeping only a core group for the duration.

—Schedule a 15-minute committee meeting before a lengthier staff meeting.

—To enhance contributions from those who attend, request that people bring, study, or look into certain agenda issues before the meeting. Make your assignments specific: Mary reports on the latest sales figures; John reports on the sales outlook, etc. Or have them meet in pairs to undertake a specific assignment on which they'll report. You'll heighten attention because they know they are accountable.

- **When** you schedule a meeting can affect how promptly people arrive as well as how promptly they are willing to leave:

  —To encourage people to work through the agenda efficiently, schedule a meeting just before lunch or at 4:30 P.M.

  —Many companies like to have staff or department meetings early in the week. Try Monday at 11:00 A.M. to give employees the first couple of hours of the work week to get their own priorities in order.

  —Avoid scheduling meetings on Friday afternoon.

- If your office is using computer networks with scheduling software, you can save time when setting up a meeting. The computer program can determine a mutually convenient time for all who should attend and send each an advisory of the meeting; it also requests confirmation of the intent to attend.

- **Where** to hold a meeting? For maximum efficiency:

  —Avoid meeting in a restaurant where the atmosphere is noisy and casual. Look for a conference room or an office instead.

—Avoid using your own office. If you meet in a conference room, you can walk out at the conclusion of the meeting. If the group has gathered in your office, it can take extra time to move everyone out.

SETTING UP
THE AGENDA

- For any formal meeting, an agenda should always be prepared.
- For a large or extensive gathering, circulate to the committee in charge a preliminary agenda for comments.
- Once the agenda is set, all people attending the meeting should receive it in advance. If the agenda has reading material attached, be sure that participants receive it in plenty of time.
- The agenda should:
  —Specify a time that the meeting will start and end
  —Outline specifically what is to be resolved
  —Schedule the most important items first
  —Bring forward items from past meetings for follow-up (people will take meetings more seriously if they know there is follow-through)
- Create a standing agenda to use for groups that meet daily or weekly: the upcoming schedule, discussion of major clients, pressing issues, etc.

RUNNING AN EFFICIENT MEETING

- At the time the meeting is to begin, close the door and start, whether or not you have a full group. If you have people who are chronically late, speak to them privately afterwards.

- The first few minutes of a meeting set the tone. Review the agenda; stress that you intend to run on schedule, and that a specific—and limited—amount of time will be given to all issues.

- Assign roles to increase involvement:

  —Appoint a facilitator who keeps the meeting moving by keeping track of and summarizing key points, acknowledging the contributions of participants, and ending the meeting on time. This works best when the job of facilitator is rotated.

  —Have a recorder take minutes, if necessary. This provides an organized method for keeping track of the meeting's action items, deadlines, and names of people responsible for various post-meeting assignments.

- Keep it interesting:

  —Vary the pace of a long meeting. Invite outside guests to speak if they will clarify issues and further the meeting's goals.

  —Use a flip chart or an overhead projector for keeping key points visible to everyone.

—Keep the discussions on the topic; take control if the conversation begins to wander.

- Discussing a complicated issue? Break into work groups, each with a specific goal.

- If the goal of your meeting is to brainstorm, identify and state the problem. Then have someone record all the suggestions on a flip chart or chalkboard. Set a time limit on the brainstorming so that there is still time during the meeting to choose one to three ideas for further exploration or implementation.

- If you will be introducing an idea that will mean a radical change, talk it over with a few colleagues ahead of time so that the entire group isn't caught by surprise. You'll have a better outcome if a few people understand your intent and can support you.

- For better people management at meetings:

  —Those who tend to remain quiet should be asked for their opinions.

  —Those who dominate meetings may need to be told: "We have a limited amount of time today. Could I ask that only those who haven't spoken yet address the group now."

- Meetings tend to wander when people:

  —Gossip or chat. Counter with: "We'll need to move ahead . . ."

  —Bring up unrelated experiences. If the speaker gets off the topic, encourage him or her to stick with the discussion at hand.

—Have a major disagreement. These usually can't be resolved at a meeting. If one erupts, it will have to be discussed privately.

- Try to reach some type of decision on each agenda item. Assign responsibility at the time if action needs to be taken.

- Use an index card system for keeping track of delegated tasks. As each task is discussed and assigned, fill out the index card (*see below*).

WORTH THE TIME

Then let someone in your department follow up on the assignments shortly before the next meeting to be certain everything gets done. Try putting a stack of blank index cards at various points along the meeting table. Staff members who don't bring their daily planner or electronic calendar with them may use the cards to note down their own assignments.

Task	Person to Whom Assigned	Date due

- Recap what took place at the meeting; don't end on a vague note. If the issues were complex, send out a follow-up memo of the minutes.

- If there is to be another meeting, announce it at the end of the meeting and send an e-mail reminder.

- End the meeting on time.

A TTENDING A MEETING

- If you've been notified of a meeting you are to attend, first consider:

  —Is it the type of meeting where your company or department needs to be represented, but not necessarily by you? If possible, send a surrogate.

  —If the meeting is likely to be lengthy and you are needed for only a couple of agenda items, consider attending for only the sections that are appropriate for you.

- Here are three ways to keep track of meeting materials:

  1. In your calendar next to the notation of the meeting, keep a list of papers or items you are to bring.

  2. Start a file for materials for each type of meeting you attend ("Compensation," "Company Planning," etc.). As the week or

month goes by, put into the folder all that you'll need for the up-coming meeting.

3. Ask your secretary or assistant to collect materials for you and file them for the day of the meeting.

- If you will be making a presentation, be prepared. Even a two-minute report deserves a few notes jotted down so that you cover the material in a logical sequence and don't leave anything out.

- If you're caught in the midst of a meeting where points are discussed with no resolution, try asking: "Before we leave this topic, could we firm up what we're going to do?"

- If you regularly have to attend a meeting that is handled poorly, offer to take notes. This gives you permission to interrupt and pin down a decision on a regular basis. "Before we go on, I need to clarify for the notes what the next step will be."

- Always carry with you something to do (mail to answer? articles to read?), so that if the meeting is delayed, you're in control of your waiting time.

ENDING THE ONE-ON-ONE MEETING

■ If you are in your office and meeting one-on-one with someone, here are some suggestions for drawing the meeting to a close:

—State in advance that your time is limited: "I've got a meeting downstairs in ten minutes."

—Get up and offer your hand, or start walking toward the door.

—Ask that a secretary or colleague notify you at a specific time. This provides you with an opportunity to end the meeting if you need to.

—If you must end the meeting, but issues are still unresolved, offer to get back to them at a mutually convenient time.

■ If a person comes into your office seeking an impromptu meeting, you might be able to accomplish two goals at the same time. If you're on the way to another meeting, invite the person to walk along with you to discuss the issue that concerns them. Or, if you have an errand to do, you might try: "I was just on my way across the street. Can we talk about it while we walk?"

PART FOUR

SPACE

MANAGEMENT

11

THE DESK

WHAT'S AHEAD

When it comes to desk management, most people employ the ever popular "pile management" system. On client visits, I see desk after desk with papers spread out; piles tipping over; stacks teetering precariously . . . rarely a work surface in sight!

Most aspiring organizers tell me they are *afraid* to put things away for fear they will forget to do it. The result is desk chaos, with no room for distraction-free work.

So, if *your* desk looks like an archaeological dig because there are so many layers of civilization to uncover and:

- Co-workers are afraid to leave something with you
- You've misplaced some papers this week—again
- You have more than three projects out and available
- You "file" your work in piles
- Things have gotten so bad you've had to "move out" of your office to find new work space

then keep reading!

THE DESK SET-UP

- Look for a desk that is long but not too wide. On a deep desk, papers, file folders, and other paraphernalia tend to get lost on the back. A broad surface offers you the ultimate in accessibility while you're working.

- Tools and accessories that *belong* on your desktop include:
  —Blotter (optional)
  —Telephone
  —Answering machine, if needed
  —Clock (or this can be hung on the wall)
  —Calendar
  —Personal address book or telephone number roll-file
  —Pencil holder containing:

    Pens

    Pencils

    Scissors

    Ruler

    Letter opener

  —Paperclip holder
  —Stapler
  —Tape dispenser

- A good desk lamp can also make all the difference in the "feel" of your office. The incandescent light softens the desk area in offices lit by fluorescent lighting. When you choose where to place the lamp, check for shadows. Lefties need the light on their right; right-handed people do best with it on the left.

- A desk needs at least three drawers. Use drawer dividers or a drawer organizing unit so that small items can be stored neatly without being jostled around.

- Use a nearby shelf or supply closet for storing backup supplies and an inventory of stationery.

- Your computer, keyboard, and accessories belong at a separate work station, preferably just a turn of the chair away from your desk.

- A bulletin board is a terrific desk aid, as long as the notes aren't left to yellow. The bulletin board should be used for reminders that you refer to regularly—zip or area code maps; or today's reminder note to jog your memory. (Take down all temporary notes when you are finished.)

- A few personal items can add character to your desk, but they should be selected carefully. Family photos, a tasteful paperweight, or personal mementos pertaining to your industry may all be in keeping with the image you want to present. When you acquire a new knickknack, it's probably time to put one away.

DIGGING YOUR WAY OUT FROM UNDER...

If your desk is buried in paper, then you need to set aside time to "dig" your way through.

- Ideally, set aside at least one hour for your first session. If you've been procrastinating on this, then start with five to ten minutes just to prove that you can make a dent in the backlog. Start with

THE THREE DRAWERS AND THEIR CONTENTS

■ In your top drawer keep:

—Calculator —Correcting fluid

—Eraser —Hole puncher

—Rubber bands —Stamps

—Staples

■ A small supply of the following belongs in a lower drawer:

—Envelopes

—Envelope labels

—File labels

—Notepaper

—Stationery (store within a file folder or in a specially designed organizing unit for stationery)

—Sticky-backed pads of the sizes you use

■ In some desks, the bottom drawer is designed to be large enough to serve as a small file drawer. If so, this space is just right for holding "active" projects. A narrow standing file holder may fit into the drawer to keep everything in place.

the top layer (most recent?) first. Process (toss, file, or act on) absolutely everything that you can.

- When you have only 15 minutes left during this session, try to bring order to the papers remaining. Group letters to answer; put together items for an upcoming report; put all "problem items" in a large pile.

- Now you'll need a box and some temporary file folders to hold these leftover papers until they can be placed where they belong permanently. Label the files according to the groups of paper you've created ("Financial," "Letters to Answer," "Problem Pile," etc.). Put the papers in the files, and the files into the box. At subsequent work sessions, you will continue sorting through these papers, either acting on them or placing them in permanent files. (See Chapter 7, "Files," for information on setting up permanent files.)

- Schedule a second session to continue working through this backlog until you've completed the task at hand.

- Once you've successfully unburied your desk, use the suggestions below to keep it well organized.

DESK MANAGEMENT: ACTIVE PAPERWORK

- Every time you start a project, reach for a file folder and label it. Even the project that must be done within 24 hours needs a folder.

THE "PROBLEM" PILE

Everyone has a "problem" pile. Set aside a block of time when you plan to address it. Go through and evaluate what to do with each paper:

- **You can toss it.** By the time papers have been left to "age," this "items to toss" category can be quite large. I've helped clients finally resolve to toss: notes for good ideas—or ideas that would have worked if the client had acted on them a month ago; reading material that would have been fascinating if it had been done before the information went out of date; letters that are no longer relevant and therefore not worth answering.

- **You can act on it.** This may mean making a phone call, writing a letter, or starting a new project.

- **You can file it.** Create a new file if necessary. If it's something you really intend to do but can't right now, put it in a "Tickler" file for the time when you expect to do it.

- Three handy "active" files that you may find convenient include:

  1. **A "To Copy" file.** You needn't hop up to photocopy a just-completed letter or report. Place all pages to be copied in this file. Do the copying—or have it done—at the end of your work session.

  2. **A "To Enter" file.** This file is for all those slips and scraps on which you've noted information you want to enter into your computer. It's a time-waster to keep interrupting other work to

record a new entry in your financial records or to add a name and address to your files; place these notes to yourself within this file and catch up at the end of each day.

3. A "Take Home" file. Some people keep their briefcase beside their desk so it's right there for the "Take Home" items. Others prefer transferring a "home" file folder to their briefcase at the end of the day.

- Active, ongoing projects need to be accessible (but not so accessible that you stack them on your desk!). If your desk has a file drawer built into it, place active projects in that drawer. If your desk drawers aren't large enough to accommodate a file, then purchase a graduated-step file holder in which to store active files. Try to keep this on a credenza or bookshelf near your desk, but not on it.

- Afraid you'll forget about it, once the project is filed? Keep track of your on-going projects by writing them down in one of these three places:

WORTH THE TIME

1. In your computer. Many business people use the new software that reminds them of tasks left undone from previous days or sets off alarms when it's time to make a phone call. It's also a perfect place to keep tabs on major projects.

2. In your calendar. Your appointment calendar is an ideal place for keeping a list of what needs to be done for various projects.

3. On your Master List. (See Chapter 2, "Get It Done!")

- When "active" files cease being active (when the project is complete), remove them from your immediate desk area and store them with your regular files.

DESK MANAGEMENT: REMINDER PAPERS

- Reminder papers are documents providing you with specific information on which you intend to act. Generally, you can transfer the information (time of meeting, date of reception, etc.) to your calendar and toss the paper. If you need to RSVP, do so immediately, then transfer the information.

- If you need travel directions or an agenda at a later date, you will need to file it. If you have a file on the upcoming meeting, then put the directions or agenda within this file. Otherwise, drop the paper into your "Tickler" file for the upcoming date.

DESK MANAGEMENT: REFERENCE ITEMS

Reference materials all need to have a proper place so that they are accessible to you again and again.

- Your calendar and address book belong on your desk for at-a-glance reference.

- Books should be placed on a nearby shelf.

- If your reference materials are magazine articles or loose papers, create files for them. A specific project might merit two file folders: one to hold the active work you're performing, the other labeled "Background" or "Research" to hold the reference materials to which you refer.

- There are several possibilities for the business cards you are given:

  1. Transfer the information to your address book or computer, and throw out the card.

  2. If you use a roll-file system for telephone number retrieval, attach business cards to the roll cards for easy reference.

  3. Purchase one of the specially made folders designed for collections of business cards (these are available at office supply stores). You can categorize or file alphabetically within.

DESK MANAGEMENT: READING MATERIALS

- All reading materials should be categorized and assigned a time when you will read them. The "when" may make a difference as to where you place the materials. For example:

  1. The business magazine that you intend to read on the train ride home should go in your briefcase.

2. The monthly report you plan to go through next week when you're out of town should go in the file of materials you are setting aside for next week's trip.

3. The material for an upcoming meeting should be placed in a "Reading" file. Carry this file with you, and if you don't get it done in a day or two, assign a specific time to complete the reading before the upcoming meeting.

- If you're really behind in your reading, you'll need to set aside an afternoon for going through and catching up.

- Toss what you know you'll never get around to.

IMPROVING YOUR DESK WORK HABITS

- Don't let papers pile up. Process each piece of paper as it comes in. (See Chapter 8, "The Mail.")

SMART TIP

- Always re-file what you take out.

- Set aside time daily for doing paperwork. Come in early, stay late (if it's quiet), or ask your secretary to hold calls (or trade telephone coverage with a colleague) so that you can get things done.

- If you have a secretary, an "in" and "out" basket are just fine, but place these baskets so that you can't see them while you're working at your desk. (It's too easy to become distracted by the mail or something new that has just come in.)

- If you do not have a secretary or assistant, you've got to fully process what is coming in and out of your office. Select a place (off your desk) for outgoing mail. (See Chapter 8, "The Mail," for other processing ideas.)

A FINAL RULE THAT SHOULD NEVER BE BROKEN

- Clean off your desk at the end of each day. Tidy up, re-file what you had out, and put away whatever you were working on.

- Once your desk is clear, select your priority project for the next day and put it right on the front of your desk before leaving. By knowing what your first task is, you'll get a running start the next morning.

You'll soon find that starting the next day with an uncluttered desk and a clear mind will boost your productivity.

12

WORK SPACE

WHAT'S AHEAD

The Ideal Office
Storage Space
Office Supplies: Don't Run Out

Your office is your "home away from home," but few people take the time to *really* make it comfortable. Take a look around. Does your office space work for you?

—Do you have separate space for storage and for work?

—Are your frequently used items close at hand?

—Where is the equipment located? (Your constantly used computer should be right by you; a copier used daily should be down the hall.)

—Is your office layout distracting? Do you find yourself watching the passing parade that goes by? Are you often interrupted by the hallway conversations that you overhear?

—Is a visitor comfortable in your office?

—Do you have the right space for different types of work within your office (one-on-one meetings; larger get-togethers)?

If you answered no to even one of these questions, then you need to learn how to arrange furniture, equipment, and supplies for maximum efficiency.

THE IDEAL OFFICE

- **Chair.** A swivel-style desk chair should be the pivotal item in your work environment. All other items you use frequently should be accessible from it. The chair you choose should be comfortable, offering good lower back support, and the height should be set so that your thighs are parallel to the floor when your feet are resting on the floor.

- **Desk.** The shape of your office may dictate the placement of the desk. However, most people like the desk positioned in the center of the office with the doorway peripherally visible (not so that you're staring out of it). This permits gracious greeting of guests without catching the eye of everyone who passes by.

- **Computer table.** Today, almost everyone wants or needs a computer near at hand. To the left of your desk (if you're right- handed) should be a table for your computer and its accessory items. A *copy stand* is an ideal way to organize the materials from which you're working. Look for one that features a mobile "arm" and a base that rests beneath the computer terminal. This offers maximum convenience and takes up a minimum of space.

- **Credenza.** If you have the space, place a credenza behind your desk (a half-swivel from your desk/work surface). The closed storage beneath permits easy access to a variety of items that are better off out of view (extra desk supplies, publication storage, etc.). The tabletop surface permits placement of standing files or an "in/out" box to free up desk space. However, if you can't resist stacking piles of paper on the credenza, replace it with a two-drawer lateral file system. Then you can keep all those "stacks" at your fingertips, but stored neatly in files.

- **File cabinets.** These can be placed within your office as space and need permit. If your company keeps most files in a file room, a small file unit should serve your needs. (See Chapter 7, "Files," for more information.)

- **Shelves.** These are necessary for reference books and other items, but don't use them for stacking things! It's unsightly, and stacks of papers on shelves are as bad as those stacked on your floor or desk.

- **Visitor seating.** You'll want the visitor's chair placed to one side of the desk or directly opposite you across the desk. Situate it so that neither of you will need to move furniture in order to chat comfortably. To test: Try "visiting" your own office. Walk in and try out the visitor's chair for comfort. Make certain it's not so deep that you have to struggle to get back up from it. In addition, some offices may have room for larger groups of visitors:

—**Couch and comfortable armchair.** This type of seating can be useful for executives who favor a more relaxed atmosphere for meetings.

—**Conference table.** In an oversized office, this creates a comfortable seating area for meetings, and it lets your desk remain a more private work space since people won't be milling around it.

—**Vertical wall storage unit.** (*See right*) If you have limited space because your desk is in an open cubicle or a "bay," consider wall units (shallow file units that fasten to a wall) for vertical paper management.

—Wastebasket. One of the best organizing tools in your office! If your office is large, you may want two (put one right by your desk).

STORAGE SPACE

Supplies can be broken down into two categories:

1. Items you use frequently (pens, calculator, stationery, envelopes, etc.) and to which you should have easy access. (*See Chapter 11, "The Desk," for storage ideas for these items.*)

2. Backup supplies ranging from boxes of extra pens and new file folders to computer supplies and toner for the copier.

(*See below for suggestions on storing these supplies.*)

- Group supplies by type: all computer supplies together; copier supplies on a shelf of their own, etc.

- Select placement of supplies based on frequency of usage. Backup supplies needed more frequently (envelopes?) should be placed so that they are accessible; ribbons for an infrequently used typewriter should go on a less easily accessible shelf.

- If supplies are stored up high, a kick stool should be kept in the closet.

- Label shelves; use color-coding when you can. (Color-code by supply type, or if several people share a storage area, by person or by department.)

- Ask that the company purchase a few office organizers (stacking paper trays, holders, etc.) that will help keep the supplies in good order. A few home organizers, such as a lazy Susan (spinning caddy), can make small items such as correcting fluid bottles easier to reach.

- If you need to keep back issues of magazines or trade publications on hand for reference, requisition special magazine files so that you don't save in stacks. Also determine a "no longer needed" date when the publications can be moved to "dead" storage or tossed. (See Chapter 7, "Files," for additional information.)

- Doctors, dentists, and anyone who operates out of multiple offices should organize the storage areas in each room so they are exactly the same. Then, no matter which office you're in, the supplies can be found in the same place.

OFFICE SUPPLIES: DON'T RUN OUT!

- Every supply cabinet should have a "shopping list" that is managed so that the supplies are never totally depleted. The key here is noting down items when the company is low, not out:
  - Post a "To Order" list on the back of the supply cabinet door and ask that people use this to note down needed items; or
  - Create a slip that can be filled out and left in an envelope tacked to the door.

- Establish a routine time for placing supply orders so that employees become accustomed to when supplies will be replenished.

- Information on frequently ordered items should be listed on the computer of the person who places the orders. With a touch of a key, he or she has easy access to order numbers, past price, and the company from whom to order. (This way even an office temporary could place an order.) One day soon, much of the ordering done by businesses will be done via the Internet, further saving time and effort in placing an order.

- Many printing companies place a reorder slip toward the bottom of boxes of invoices, checks, etc. Use this system with other types of supplies. If you're stacking up six boxes of letterhead stationery, or four boxes of toner, tape a "remember to order" slip on the next to-last box so that someone will see it before the supply is depleted.

13

YOUR OFFICE AT HOME

WHAT'S AHEAD

What You Need to Do First

Setting Up Your Space

The Telephone

Equipping Your Office

What to Do When Your Equipment
Goes Down

Furniture

Supplies

Managing Your Time

A client called me with a desperate plea for help. Her home office was just not working out. I soon agreed, after learning that her business day started only after her morning ritual ended: First, she took the dog for a nice long walk; then she watched the morning news programs, had a hearty breakfast, and read the newspaper cover to cover. . . . By the time she finished, it was approaching noon!

Her work station was a cart by her bed with files stuffed in a hall linen closet. There was no second telephone line, so anyone in the household could answer the phone—including her two-year-old. And because everyone knew she was home, family and friends considered her their "errand lady."

Step one in helping her remedy her situation was teaching her to treat her home office like a real business. I helped her establish less erratic hours, a proper filing and telephone system, and we created a place where she could really work.

Working from home is a new American dream, but once there, you may find there's no fax machine, you've run out of pens, the phone call is Junior who needs a ride, and there's no one (over age twelve) to chat with during the day.

All those problems can be solved if you take time to set up an efficient home office. The advantages? You'll have the best of both worlds. You'll be able to balance personal life and career, and there will be no traffic delays or commuting time. As your business grows, you'll find that investing in yourself was the best thing you've ever done.

WHAT YOU NEED TO DO FIRST

- Consult an attorney regarding any business filings or details that might need to be taken care of in order to set up a business. Check with an accountant who can help you meet all IRS requirements.

- Create your tax categories at the beginning of each year and keep them recorded regularly.

- If you're just starting a home business, open a separate checking account to keep business expenses and personal expenses separate. Open a savings account, too, to put away funds for federal, state, city, and Social Security taxes.

- Isolation is a common problem for home-based business owners. Keep up contacts by joining professional organizations and attending meetings out.

Important!

SETTING UP YOUR SPACE

To decide how best to set up your home office, consider the exact nature of your work and write down your requirements:

WORTH THE TIME

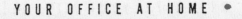

- What types of tasks will you be performing (computer work, drafting, drawing, sewing, telephoning)?

- What furniture and equipment will you need to do this work (drafting table, desktop publishing equipment, storage cabinets, bulletin board)?

- Do you have a product that must be stored and/or sent out? You'll need room for storage, and you'll have to carve out space for packing and materials.

- What else must be accommodated in the room? Partners, secretaries, assistants, salespeople?

- Will clients or customers come to your home?

- Check the zoning for your neighborhood. Storage of certain types of business materials, parking, the comings and goings of customers and/or employees, a separate business entrance, and the amount of the home devoted to the business are all areas that might require the approval of a local zoning board.

- If you don't have an extra bedroom or den, be creative. With your requirements in mind, try to visualize where you might carve out the space you need. A nook, a large walk-in closet, or a corner of another room, preferably partitioned by a full or halfwall or a decorative screen, can provide an efficient work space. Or can a section of the basement, garage, or attic be renovated? (Consider heating and cooling problems if you are thinking of making one of these areas habitable.)

- Select a space that can be totally devoted to your business. A separate work place helps you have a "work" life and a "home" life, and it's also important to the IRS. Under current tax laws, you need a room solely dedicated to business to qualify for the home-office tax deduction. Check with your accountant if you're not sure your space qualifies. Maybe there are simple modifications you can make.

- If possible, try to set up your home office in a part of the home that is off the family path.

- If clients or customers do come, avoid an office near the bedrooms, and consider whether you'll have enough traffic that you'll need a waiting area or a separate entrance. If you'd prefer to meet clients on neutral ground, find a restaurant or a nearby hotel with a quiet lobby (many have coffee and tea service) in which to hold one-on-one meetings or small get-togethers.

- Consult with an electrician. If you're adding a computer and fax machine, you almost certainly need additional outlets, and an electrician can ground your computer to lessen the possibility of computer problems caused by power outages.

- For a fax machine and modem, you'll need to add extra telephone jacks.

THE TELEPHONE

Your home-office telephone system should feature:

- **A separate line for the business:**

   —A separate line for business allows you to "close" for the weekend by letting a machine cover the business line.

   —Children can be prevented from functioning as "operator" if you give them specific directions as to which line they should not answer. (With toddlers, you'll have to keep any telephone with a business line out of reach.)

   —A second line permits you to make outgoing personal calls on your "home" line, leaving the business line free for incoming calls.

   —For a fee, you can ask for Call Waiting. When you are on a call and don't want to be interrupted, you can utilize "Cancel Call Waiting," which permits you to deactivate the service during important conversations.

   —An extra line for fax/modem hook-up. Fax machines are becoming almost as common as telephone answering machines, and every small business owner should have access to the Internet. The Web is making it easy for the "little guy" to compete right alongside the corporate giants, but you have to be wired in to know what's going on. And no business can afford to get along without e-mail, so you'll need the modem for e-mail as well.

- **An answering machine or voice-mail service:**

  —Answering machines have become much more sophisticated, permitting callers to leave messages in a "home box" or an "office box," depending on the line they have called. Your computer can function as a voice-mail service, though it takes up a great deal of disk space.

  —Or consult your phone service. Companies are now offering voice-mail services for the home user that can take messages while you're on the phone or when you're away.

  —On your voice-mail system or answering machine, record a business-oriented message that runs consistently. Unless you're running a birthday party service or a toy company, your children should not do the recording.

- **Appropriate "extras":**

  —You can buy telephones with conference-call capabilities, redial services, and the technology to speed-dial certain numbers.

  —Ask the phone company about Call Forwarding and intercom possibilities.

  —With prices and special promotions being offered on 800 numbers, those services, too, are now within the reach of the home-based entrepreneur.

- **A mute button:**

    —The dog barks or the toddler wails? Use your "mute" button. You can still hear the person on the other end of the phone, yet you can block sound from your home office until you can cut in to say: "Could you hold for a moment, please?"

E QUIPPING YOUR OFFICE

- Telecommuters on a company payroll should negotiate with the company for a fully equipped office.

- If you're just starting a business, set your priorities. Business equipment must take priority over furniture. Clients don't care whether your work is done at a mahogany desk or at one from a secondhand store, but they do care about the appearance of the work you'll produce for them.

- Most home-based businesses will need:

    —Computer with extra storage capacity (if you'll interface electronically with a client, be certain your equipment is compatible)

    —Laser printer

    —Modem

    —Fax machine or fax/modem

—Copier (invest in one when you realize your trips to the copy shop are taking up too much of your work time)

—Postage scale and meter

—Slide or overhead projector, if needed

- Purchase a surge protector. For the dollars spent, it guards against computer data loss.

ANTICIPATE THE WORST

WHAT TO DO WHEN YOUR EQUIPMENT GOES DOWN

1. Call the appropriate 800 numbers for support. Some amazing malfunctions can be solved by phone.
2. If possible, buy from dealers who will lend you equipment while yours is being serviced. (Even if there is a rental fee, it's worth it.)
3. Make agreements with colleagues with compatible systems. If your computer is down, arrange to use theirs in a pinch; return the favor if needed.
4. When you upgrade, hold on to your equipment (if space allows). You can revive the old system if you're desperate.
5. Consider buying back-ups for your printer or computer. Take advantage of sales and price drops for certain pieces of equipment.

- If you travel, you may want a laptop computer. Shop for one with a clear display screen, expanded memory, and an internal modem. A portable printer weighing between 5 and 10 pounds may also be worth the investment.

- While your computer and accessories should be new (they outdate so quickly), consider buying other equipment secondhand. Reconditioned office copiers (far superior to those created for home use) can generally be purchased from a dealer at a fraction of what they would cost new, and by purchasing secondhand you may be able to afford time-saving features such as a sheet feeder and document sorter.

- When buying equipment, ask about special promotions or buying incentives in addition to negotiating selling prices. There are generally ways to get a discount or a free add-on along with your primary purchase.

FURNITURE

- Look at office furniture catalogs or visit showrooms to get a feel for the prices.

- Built-in furniture can offer the most efficiency in a small space and may even cost less. Measure and build around your equipment.

- Shop garage sales, auctions, used furniture and warehouse sales for desks, chairs, and tables. Filing cabinets are generally worth buying new. They'll last for years, so there's no sense in starting out with beat-up cabinets or drawers that stick.

Supplies

- Budget for office supplies. You will want to be well stocked.

- If you don't have an office supplies "supermarket" near you, then investigate catalog shopping. Several office supply companies offer fast service on discounted supplies.

MONEY SAVER

- Keep your business supplies within your home office. You shouldn't run all over the house to locate a dictionary or a hole puncher. (Don't let home accessories wander into your office either.)

TIME SAVER

- Use organizers (pencil and paperclip holders, standing file, etc.) on or near your desk to keep frequently used items neatly collected.

- Order memo pads to match your letterhead stationery so that you can dash off notes instead of always needing to do a formal letter.

MANAGING YOUR TIME

- Establish regular office hours. One of the most difficult parts about working from home is starting—and stopping.

- Some people find it helpful to "dress" for work so that they feel more businesslike. Others "go to work" by stepping out for a walk, just as if they walked to the job. When they reenter home or apartment, they know they have their "work" hat on.

- Take breaks. Find something (exercising, calling a friend) that gives you a midday break to energize you in the afternoon.

- With small children, hire a baby-sitter to take care of them. You really can't do both at the same time. For those times when the baby-sitter has left, have a backup for the after-hours business call. Stash away stickers or a favorite video tape that you can pull out for in-a-pinch entertainment.

- Keep a log of your time. (See Chapter 2, "Get It Done!") You may find that the "moments" you spent tidying up the house or weeding the garden were actually a full half hour—or more.

- When you're facing a tight deadline, turn off the phone. Monitoring the answering machine takes mental energy, and if you answer it, you're lost.

—Use a checkbook that makes carbons so that you needn't enter the information.

—Create forms of invoices and fax sheets, etc., to speed paperwork.

—Hire temporary and part-time help for chores such as envelope stuffing, product packing, filing, or mailing-list updates. Look for teens or senior citizens who need a few hours' work.

—Make use of free help where you can. A travel agent can make all trip arrangements for you; a librarian will help out on research specifics; your banker may end up being your most valuable contact since he or she can help smooth out the financial end of your business.

—At the end of each day, spend ten or 15 minutes cleaning up so that it will be easier to get going the next day.

(See Part I, Time Management, for additional information on managing your time, and refer elsewhere in the book for specifics on everything from setting up your desk to warding off procrastination.)

PART FIVE

ON THE GO

14

THE BRIEFCASE

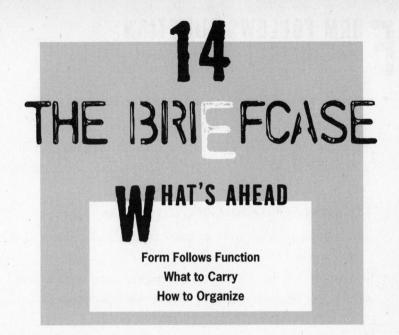

WHAT'S AHEAD

Form Follows Function
What to Carry
How to Organize

When it comes to a briefcase, it sometimes seems anything will do. One banker I know totes all of his important papers in a shopping bag or several plastic bags—whichever is more convenient that day. Another executive, an architect, carries a stunning leather briefcase— it's just that he needs a magician to open it. And one client, a theatrical agent, carries nothing: "If it doesn't fit in my pockets, I leave it at home."

If you aspire to do a bit better with your "portable office," then here's how a briefcase can work for you.

FORM FOLLOWS FUNCTION

- Features that make a briefcase an ideal carry-all:
  - —Lightweight and comfortable to carry
  - —Exterior pocket for newspaper, commuter reading material, and an umbrella
  - —Many inner compartments for supplies
  - —Closes totally, to keep papers in and rain or snow out
  - —Removable shoulder strap for travel and to make it easier to tote briefcase and other packages

- If your briefcase doesn't have compartments, use a small zippered travel bag or several transparent pouches for this purpose. Even a pencil case will do.

- Women will find that letting a briefcase double as a purse is convenient and less cumbersome than having to carry both. Add an attractive leather zippered pouch to hold toiletries, tissues, money, credit cards, and calendar. (Have a lunch appointment? Leave your briefcase at the office and take along the leather pouch.)

SMART TIP

WHAT TO CARRY

- The papers within your briefcase should all be stored within labeled file folders or envelopes.
- Carry with you:
  - —Calendar and an address book of VIP addresses and telephone numbers
  - —Pad of paper
  - —Pens, pencils, highlighter
  - —Business cards (most executives carry these in their wallets or pockets, but put a small backup supply in your briefcase).
- A few select office tools. Purchase a readymade set that includes small scissors, stapler, ruler, etc., or create your own.
- Other optional items:
  - —Stamps
  - —Sticky-backed notes
  - —Small dictaphone machine
  - —Calculator
  - —Clip-it tool for cutting out articles
  - —Several safety pins to hold loose buttons or a hem
  - —Moist towelettes

—Toothbrush

- If you travel frequently or are out of the office a great deal, keep permanently packed:

—Small amount of loose change

—Extra collar stays and socks (men) or pantyhose (ladies)

—Small supply of medicines, including a simple pain reliever, Band-Aids, antacids, and vitamins or allergy medication, if you take any (these items should be packed in a separate compartment or in their own small tote, spillproof if you carry any liquids).

HOW TO ORGANIZE

- If there is no outside pocket, newspapers can go into the briefcase folded in half. All other papers should be slipped into labeled file folders kept permanently in the briefcase: "Mail to Read," "Correspondence to Answer," and "Action Items."

- If your briefcase has two distinct compartments, designate one side a "to do" side, and the other side "done." When you arrive at the office the following day, the finished work can go directly into your assistant's basket. Make sure you sort the papers and put them in labeled file folders ("To File," "To Mail," etc.).

- Before you leave for a trip or an appointment, be certain you've packed all the appropriate materials. You can simplify this by thinking it through in advance and making notes in your calendar about what you need to take along in order to be prepared.

- Are you still writing good ideas on scraps of paper and dropping them into your briefcase? Start noting them in the extra pages of your calendar, enter them into your electronic organizer, or if these don't work for you, carry a small spiral notebook dedicated to "Ideas." When you get back to the office, be certain to add these to your Master List (see Chapter 2, "Get It Done!").

- Each evening, select what you need to take home. Better yet, store your briefcase beside your desk, and as the day goes by, slip in those items you want to look over that night. The paperwork chosen should be no more than you can reasonably expect to go through in a single evening.

- Your briefcase should be emptied nightly and cleaned out and re-supplied at least once a month.

15

BUSINESS TRAVEL

WHAT'S AHEAD

Office Preparations for Your Absence
For the Home-Based Business Owner
Trip Preparations
Preparation at Home
Packing
In Transit
While Away
Your Return

With fax machines, electronic mail, portable computers, and the telephone, business travelers are now better prepared than ever to stay in control of their workload while they are away.

But if you aspire to manage both trip and office details and still hit the ground running upon your return, there's only one way to do it: You've got to be well organized for being away—and for coming home.

OFFICE PREPARATIONS FOR YOUR ABSENCE

- Your first priority is assessing what you need while you are away:

  1. All appropriate information for client meetings or a conference you're attending should be pulled and checked to be certain that all papers are in order. Only take with you relevant documents; materials you know you won't need should be left behind. (Refile everything so you can locate it upon your return.)

  2. Also take along any files pertaining to other issues that might arise while you are away. If other clients or projects need attention, you'll want to have the proper materials with you.

  3. Now take a look at your schedule. If you have a big block of time between two meetings, or there are several free afternoons during a conference, then take along "catch up" work, or select a project—perhaps one that you just haven't been able to get around to—and pack the materials for it as well.

4. Keep all project and client files in separate, labeled folders for easy access.

- Anticipate problems that might arise and try to handle them in advance. Or explain to others what to do "if . . . "

- Streamline the process of writing up "while I'm away" instructions. Your instructions on handling the mail at the office, for example, can be put on the computer so that you need only update it for each trip.

- Delegate as much other work as possible. For your employees, prepare a list of assignments with clear instructions; for you, prepare a delegation chart so that you can keep track of what was assigned. (See Chapter 9, "Delegating.")

- Make a list of all undone tasks you can't delegate, and be certain they are on your Master List. These items will need to be added to your list of priorities when you return.

- Arrange for your secretary, assistant, or a colleague to sort through your mail, pull anything important (to handle, send, or discuss with you), and hold the remainder for your return.

Depending on the length or nature of the trip, you may want material sent to you by overnight mail (or by fax, if it's only a letter or two). Some business people routinely request that their mail be sent by overnight mail to their home, so that it can be dealt with the evening of their return, thereby clearing their morning for in-office matters.

- Also make sure someone screens and keeps track of your phone calls.

- If you'll be gone for a prolonged period of time, should clients and/or business associates be warned in advance?

- Set up a time when you will check in with the office daily, or depending on your business, two or three times per day.

- If your office needs to be able to reach you instantly, buy or lease a beeper with coast-to-coast capability.

- To prepare a portable office, you need a comfortable-to-carry briefcase with lots of compartments stocked with all the items discussed earlier, as well as your agenda and some stamps, pre-addressed overnight-mail envelopes, and files and information for the trip and other projects.

- You will also need your itinerary, tickets, legal documents (passport, driver's license, visa, etc.), travelers checks, cash, and credit cards.

- If you're traveling with a laptop computer, then invest in a special computer travel kit that can remain permanently packed. Ask at your local computer store. You may be glad to have a modem, a modular jack (if you need to connect a modem to go on-line in a hotel room), and the appropriate toll-free computer support telephone number in case you need hookup advice. If you can stay in touch via e-mail while you're away, you'll likely find any problems that might have cropped up in your absence can be easily solved.

- Take along a file or envelope for information and papers you collect on the trip (business cards, reports, fliers, receipts, and so on). Note on receipts what the expense was to simplify writing up your expense report.

FOR THE HOME-BASED BUSINESS OWNER:

■ Invest in an answering machine or voice-mail system (see Chapter 5, "The Telephone") that will permit you to pick up messages while away. Your outgoing message should provide callers with enough information that they can reach you if necessary. (One interviewer was able to track down a touring author and move up her interview time because she had left a forwarding number on her answering machine.)

■ Arrange for a family member or friend to sort the mail and let you know if anything important is going on. One business owner even arranged for a good friend to handle bank deposits to keep cash flow steady while he was away.

TRIP PREPARATIONS

- A good travel agent will prepare your tickets, get your boarding passes, and send them to you to save time at the airport. Leave a standing order with the agent as to the seat you prefer and the meal you like so that you needn't discuss these prior to each trip.

- Prepare or have your assistant prepare an itinerary of your travel plans, complete with hotel, airline, and meeting site telephone numbers. Make three copies: leave one at work, one at home, and take one with you.

- If you are trying a hotel that is new to you, ask about special services for business people. Some have executive floors with amenities such as modem hookups and better desk lighting. Other services can range from secretarial help to in-wall hair dryers and overnight pressing. If you inquire in advance, you needn't bring supplies for something the hotel provides anyway.

- If your distances are short, consider alternatives to air travel. Along the East Coast, the train from cities such as Boston, New York, Philadelphia, and Washington may be faster and easier than taking the time to travel to outlying airports.

- If you'll be renting a car at the airport, find out which company processes customers most quickly. You may have to sign up as a "special" customer to be eligible, but the time-saving benefits (speedy check-in, record-it-yourself drop-off) are worth it.

- If you're driving for any part of the trip, ask car rental companies or your auto club about computerized travel directions to your destination (or create them yourself if you have the computer program to do it).

- If this is a driving trip, shop for some of the car organizers meant to hold file papers or take along a small file box. With a portable filing system, you can carry what you need in the trunk of your car.

- Purchase a mileage logbook to record car use and mileage for tax purposes.

- If you spend a lot of time in your car, a cellular telephone is a wise investment as it enables you to return calls from the road. Shop for one with a hands-free speaker phone, and voice-activated dialing.

- As your departure date nears, confirm:

  —flight or travel arrangements

  —accommodations

  —car rental

- Take any written confirmations with you.

- Check on:

    —weather forecast as it will affect packing

    —any additional telephone numbers you might need

    —travel directions once there

- Always travel with a good supply of one-dollar bills for tipping, and a telephone credit card or ample change (if you don't have a credit card). The card simplifies expense and tax records.

- If you are traveling overseas, arrange to get some appropriate foreign currency in advance.

- If you frequently travel to the same city on business, start a file on this location. Keep information on contacts, local business groups, places and events, secrets about the city, good places to hold meetings, etc. Also file away street or subway maps and information on hotels or restaurants that you liked or want to try.

- Every frequent air traveler should have (and carry with them) a copy of the OAG Pocket Flight Guide (Official Airline Guides, 2000 Clearwater Drive, Oak Brook, IL 60521-9953; 708-574-6000). If your plane breaks down or you need to change to another connection, you can scope out for yourself what the possibilities might be.

- If you participate in a "frequent flyer" program, have on hand relevant membership numbers. You may be staying at a hotel where you can accrue additional flight miles, and you'll want to have the proper information with you.

PREPARATION AT HOME

- **If you live alone:**

  —Arrange for someone to manage mail, messages, and newspapers as well as plants and pets

  —Throw out food that will spoil while you're away

  —Let your household help know you'll be away; specify work to be performed and arrange for payment

- **If you have children:**

  —Children should be told of your trip at an age-appropriate time. Older children should be told in advance so they can plan for it; little ones should know just a day or two ahead of time

  —Those ages four and over might appreciate a tear-off calendar to count the days until your return; older children should have a copy of your itinerary

  —Confirm all child care and car-pooling arrangements for while you're away

  —Arrange a specific time to call so that you can stay in touch

- Before you walk out the door, be certain you have keys, directions, money, tickets, and itinerary.

PACKING

- Invest in a good piece of light, carry-on luggage so that you needn't check a bag. A suit-length garment bag with zippered compartments is especially practical for packing and carrying. A bigger bag must be managed in and out of the hotel, and checking and claiming luggage at the airport is a major time-waster when you're on the go.

Important!

- If you travel for long periods and carry-on luggage can't really accommodate your needs:

—Select a suitcase with wheels to facilitate getting through airports. A brightly colored bag is a good choice because it will be easy to spot. Or if your bag is a common one, put an identifying travel sticker on it to make it easy to pick out on the baggage carousel. Though your bag should be labeled, use your name and business address rather than a home address, which alerts people that you are not at home.

—In a small carry-on bag, pack toiletries, underwear, extra shirt or blouse, medication, and anything you would really need if your baggage is lost. To avoid spills, pack toiletries and medications in a leakproof bag.

- Whether you take three trips a year or thirty, prepare a toiletries kit you can leave permanently packed.

TIME SAVERS

- To pack lightly and inexpensively, buy economy-size products (lotion, shampoo, etc.) and some small plastic bottles. Transfer the products into the small containers. At the end of each trip, refill any that are getting low. Pick up travel-size toothpaste and shaving cream. Businesswomen will find that pads (instead of bottles) of makeup remover, polish remover, astringent, and cleansing pads will reduce bulk and weight for travel.

MONEY SAVER

- To create a travel medicine kit, pack aspirin, antacid tablets, anti-diarrheal medicine, Band-Aids, cough drops, decongestant, and any prescription medicines or vitamins needed. If you need corrective glasses, take a spare pair and a copy of the prescription.

- Stock up on other small, lightweight items that can also remain permanently packed, such as a travel clock, shower cap, collapsible pant or skirt hanger, lint brush, stain remover, safety pins, and sewing kit. Tuck an extra pair of socks or pantyhose and spare shoelaces in your bag.

- Write down the days you'll be gone and the clothing you'll need for each event. Select clothes with color schemes that coordinate to make several outfits. Layering will help you cope with an uncertain weather forecast, and a coat with a zip-out lining will take you through climate changes. A large shawl for female travelers will take up little room and can keep you warm in spring and fall months. Plan so that one pair of dress shoes and one pair of casual shoes will suffice. Before packing each item, double-check that it's in mint condition.

- Pack clothing as it comes from the cleaners. The tissue paper and plastic bag will protect garments from wrinkling, and you won't lose time changing hangers while unpacking.

- If you're taking a minimum of luggage and you need more than one suit, travel in one of them. A travel iron or a lightweight steamer (or a trip to the hotel pressing service) will make it presentable for your second day of meetings.

- You may also want to take recreation equipment such as a tennis racket or jogging shoes.

- Save the list of items you're packing until after the trip is over. Should your bag be lost or stolen, you'll have a record of its contents. Next time you travel, use it as a checklist.

IN TRANSIT

- Plan to arrive at the airport about an hour before flight time if you need to check a bag.

- Flight time is ideal for reviewing your notes for the upcoming meetings, catching up on business reading, or taking care of some correspondence. Prepare letters on your portable computer or by hand, or use a portable dictation machine, and send the handwritten letters, the computer disk, or the dictation tape in prestamped or overnight mail envelopes back to your office once you land.

- Membership in an airline club is a good investment for frequent travelers. It provides a comfortable place to relax during waiting time; the staff can run interference for you if a flight needs to be changed; and for travelers who want to work, space and facilities are available for spreading out or even for holding meetings. If you don't join a club, some airports have business centers where you can work.

- Don't be a victim of "waiting" time. *Choose* how you'll use unexpected time, and you'll find delays less exasperating.

WHILE AWAY

- If you've changed time zones, you may find it easier to remain mentally on your hometown time. (Change your watch to the new time zone so you don't miss appointments!) Even when the time differences are great, some business people continue to eat on a schedule more akin to their time at home—breakfast mid-morning and a light supper instead of a late dinner, for example.

- If you travel from east to west, you will likely find that you are awake earlier than your western business associates. Use the early morning hours to work in your hotel room and to keep track of business in the East by telephone.

- Mornings will go more smoothly if you order breakfast through room service the night before.

- Check in with the office at the appointed times. Return all important calls from the road, and delegate—by fax or by phone—items that come up while you're away that can be handled by someone else in the office.

- Business travel can be drudgery if you don't find a way to make it work for you. Many business people keep up with their exercise program—jogging, walking, swimming, tennis, or utilizing a hotel's exercise facilities. Others find that taking along a camera and seeking out lesser known spots gives them an interest to pursue and expands their knowledge of the new town. One business executive uses each trip as an opportunity to add to his collection of first edition books. You can also use your "away" time to accomplish errands and tasks that would take time at home. The concierge can direct you to the best place for a haircut, or you might shop for clothing so you needn't do it at home. (If you buy something, ask the store to mail it home.) By setting aside time to explore or to accomplish personal goals, you'll find the travel time much more interesting.

- Use your return flight to work on your expense report and make notes about what was accomplished during your trip. The more you can dispense with trip-related work, the better your reentry at work and home will be.

- Did you forget to pack something? Leave a note ("Remember sunglasses," or, "Don't forget stamps") in your suitcase so that you'll remember for the next time.

YOUR RETURN

No matter how well you've managed office matters from afar, there is still going to be extra paperwork, telephone messages, and people who want to see you when you return.

- Go in early or set aside a block of time on your first day back for catching up.

    —Go through any e-mail you weren't able to handle while you were away.

    —Group all telephone calls to be made.

    —As you go through the mail and papers that have come in, toss or handle with a quick handwritten reply as many of the papers as you can. Organize the remainder into categories— To Do, To File, To Read, To Call, To Delegate—and add them to your Master List of things to do.

    —You created a "To Do" list of items left pending before your departure. This list should be melded with the "To Do" items from the trip, as well as any "action" items created from the incoming mail.

    —Refer to your delegation chart and check the status of any work previously delegated.

1559

- After an absence, home life can be overwhelming, too. If you've got kids, carve out special time for them first. Otherwise, try to catch up by tackling one extra chore each evening, or treat yourself to sending out your laundry so that your first weekend home isn't lost to washing your clothing.

ABOUT THE AUTHORS

RONNI EISENBERG, author of *Organize Yourself!*, has given a multitude of workshops, lectures, and demonstrations across the country on how to get organized. She lives and works in Westport, Connecticut, with her husband and three children.

KATE KELLY, who co-authors Ronni's books, is a professional writer who owns and operates her own publishing business. She lives in Westchester County, New York, with her husband and three children.